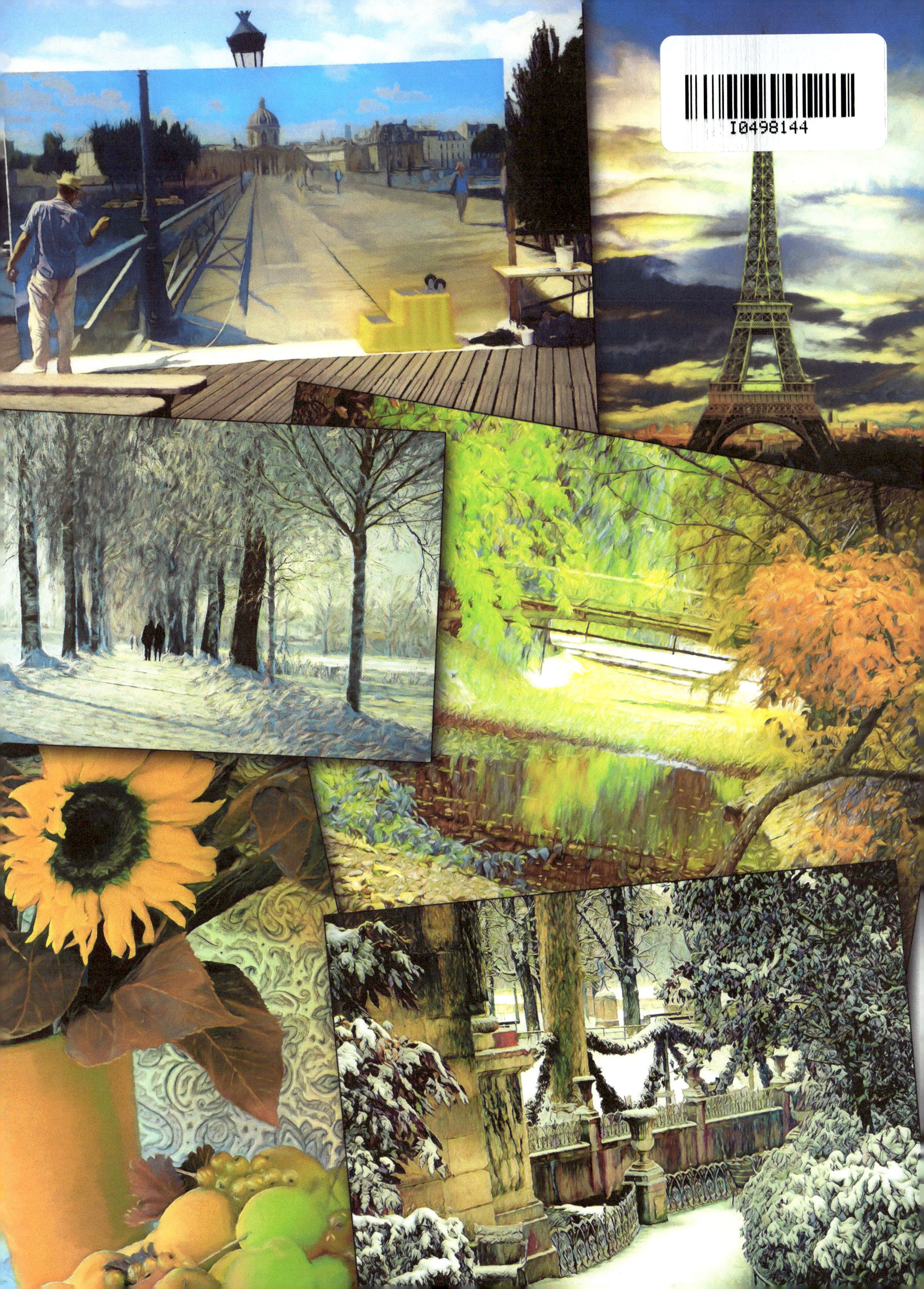

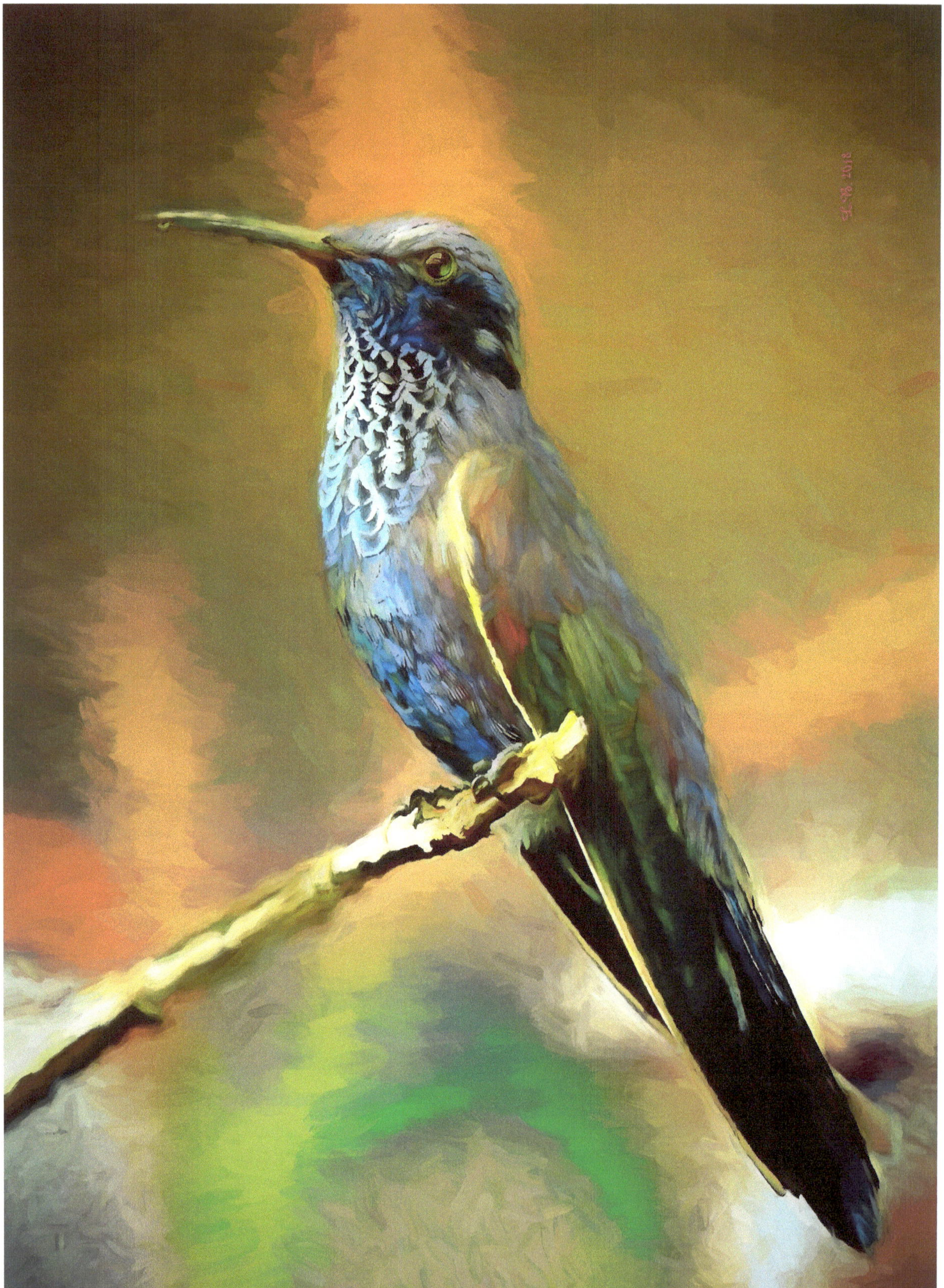

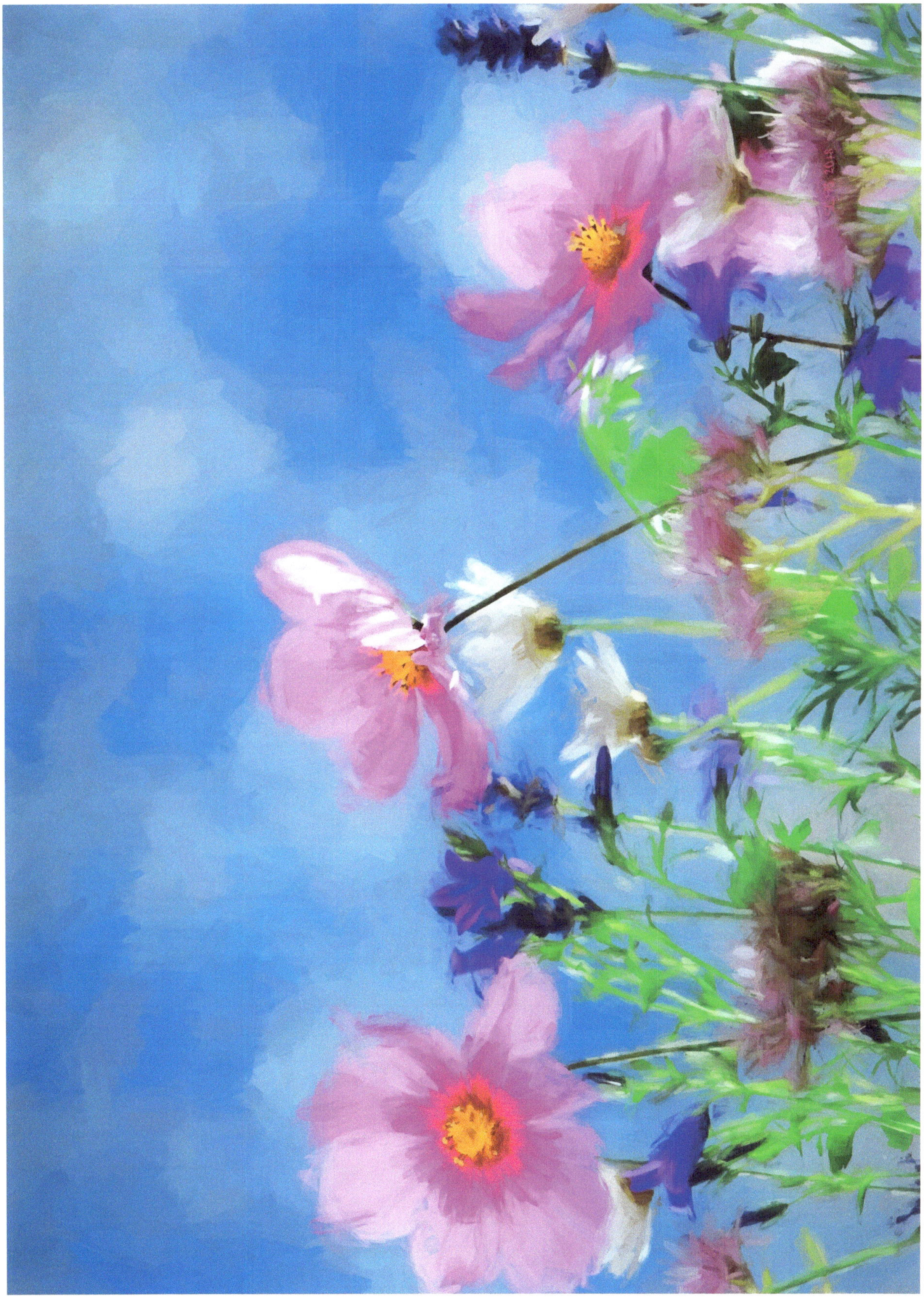

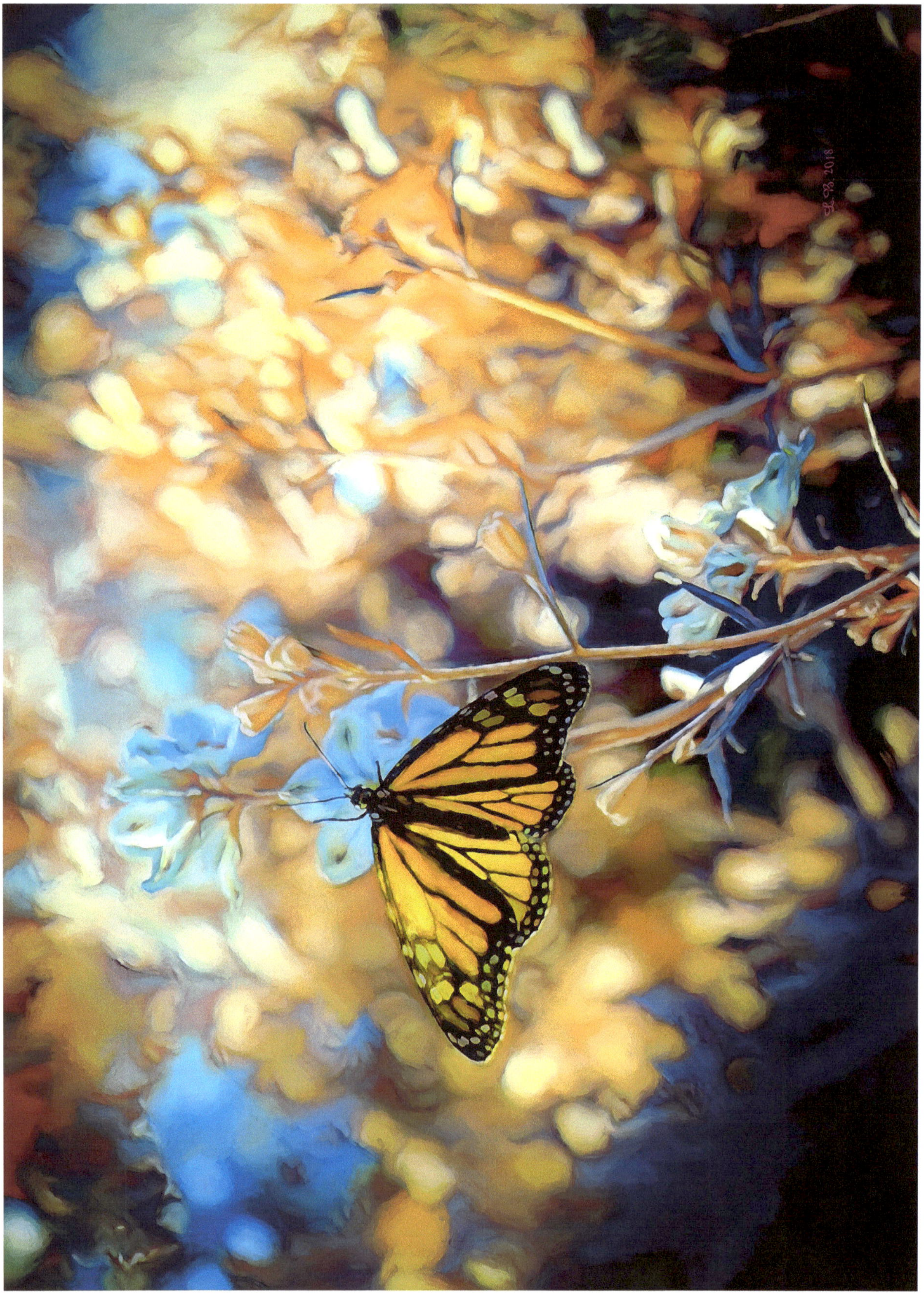

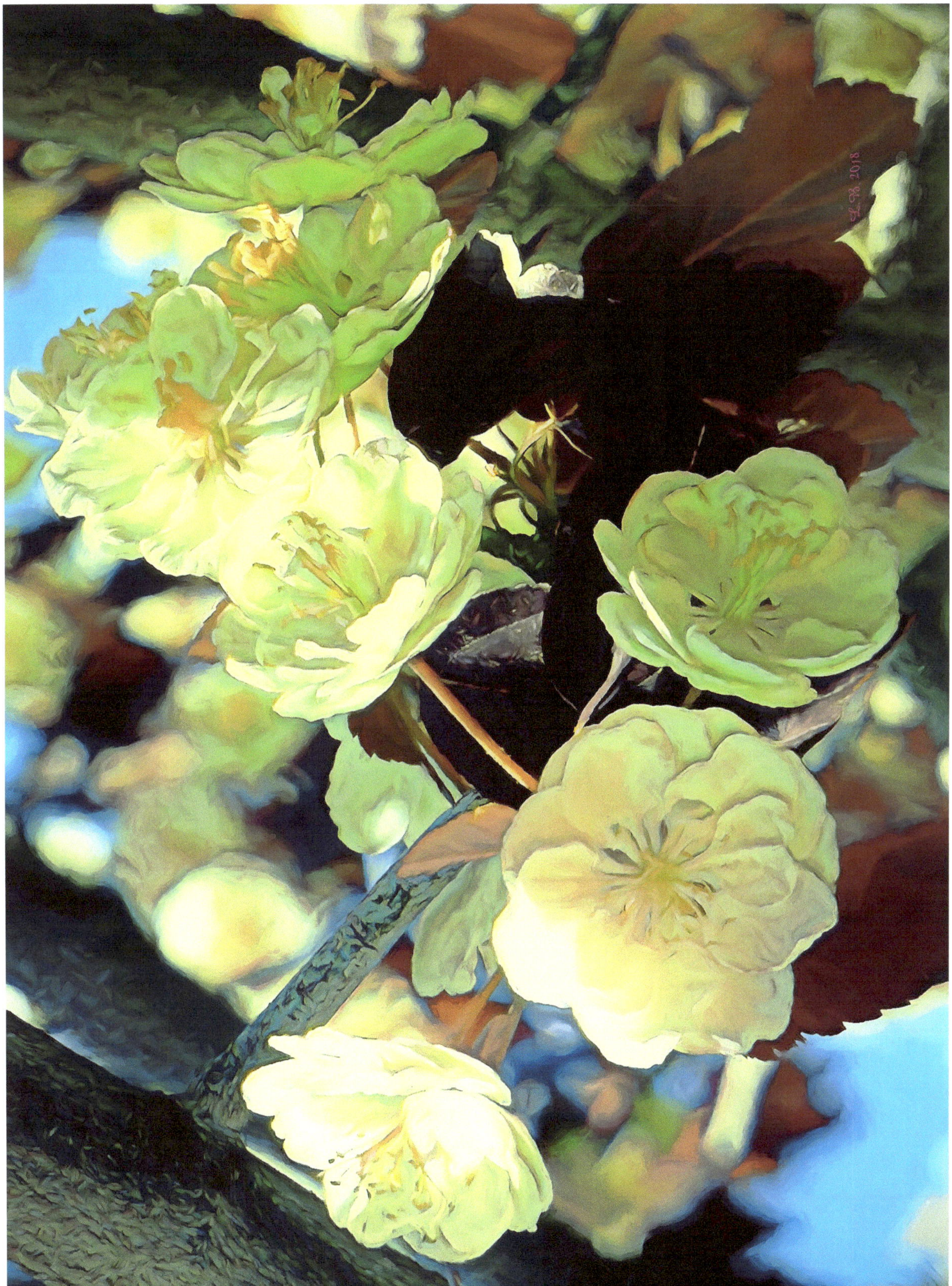

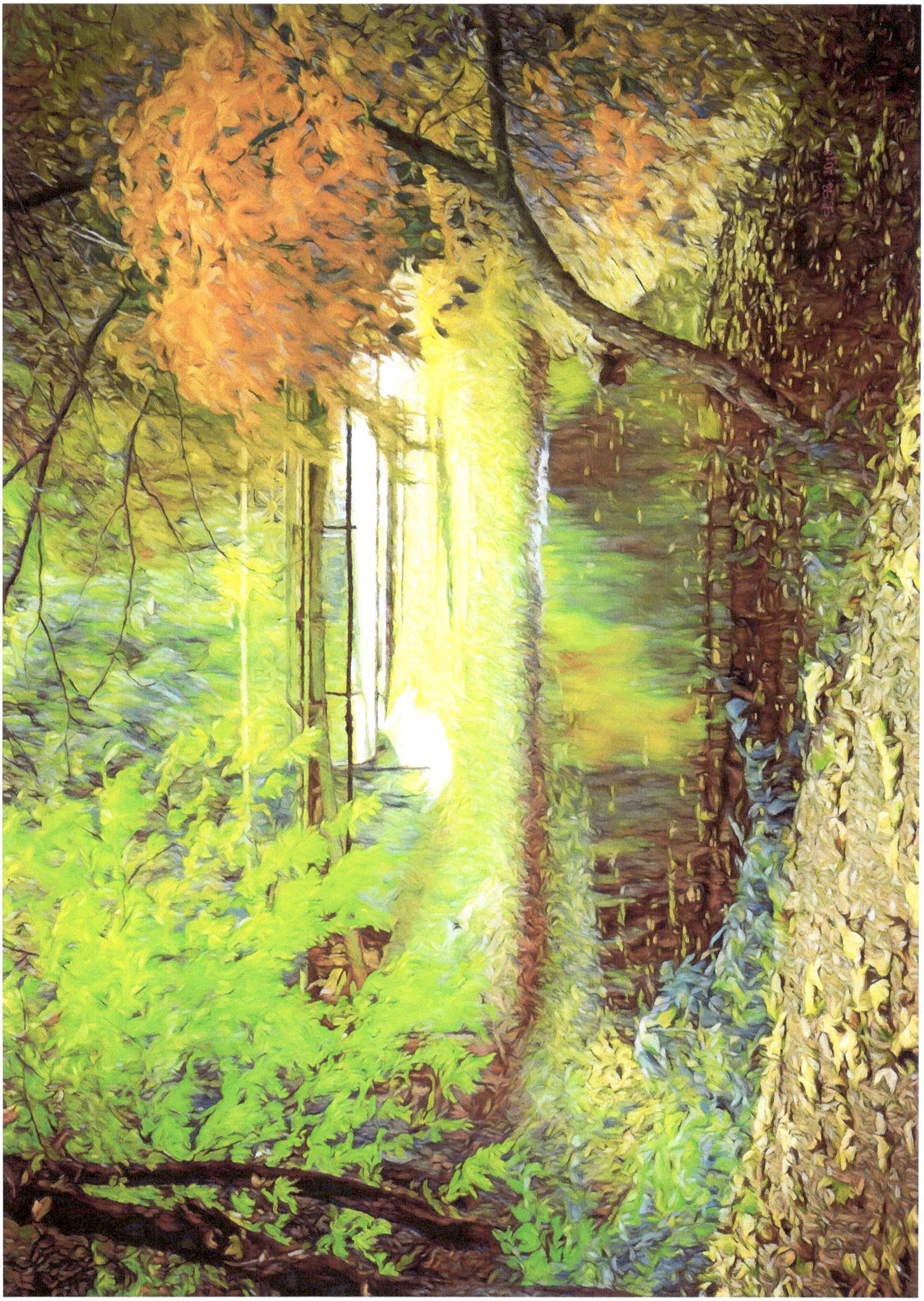

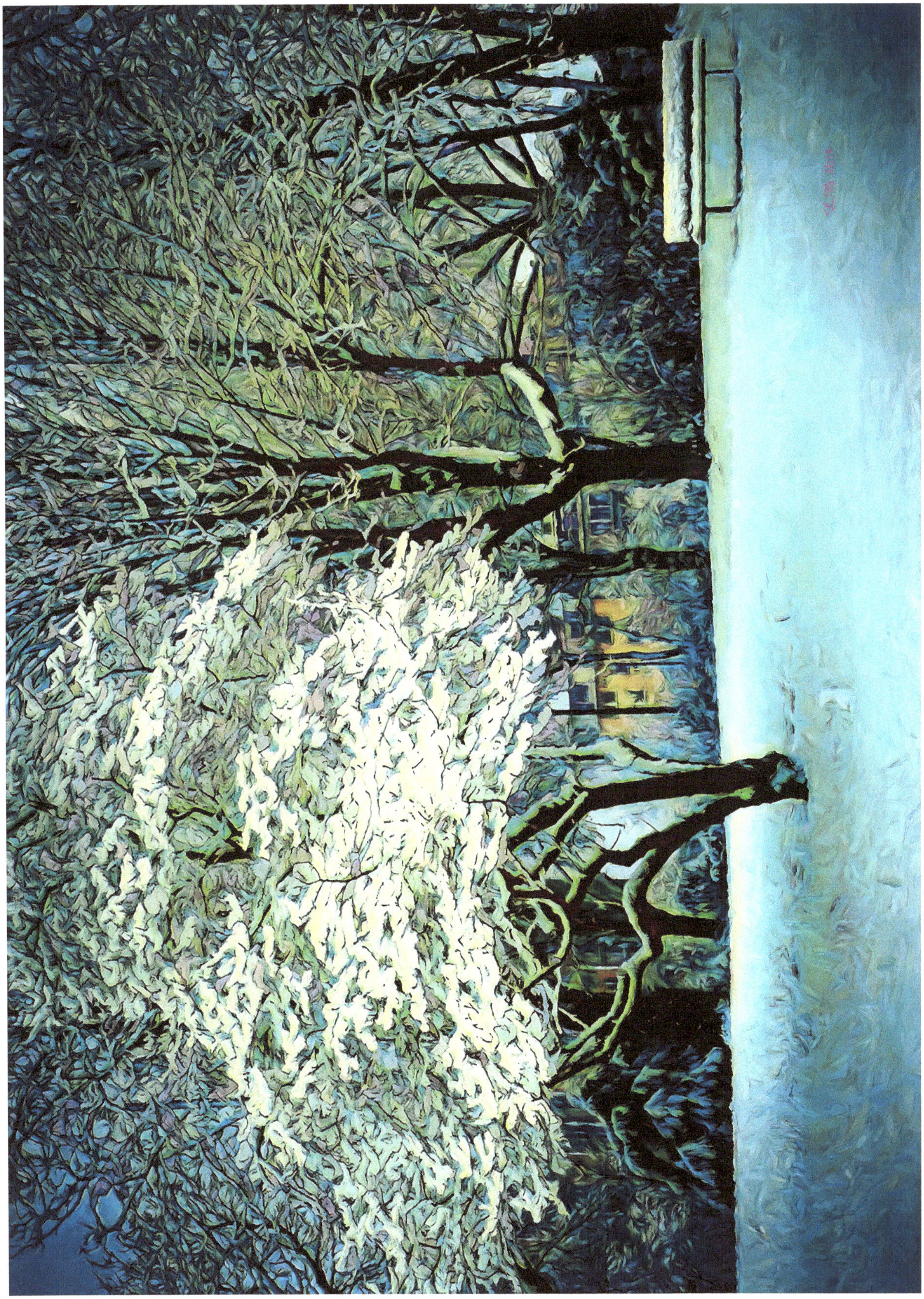

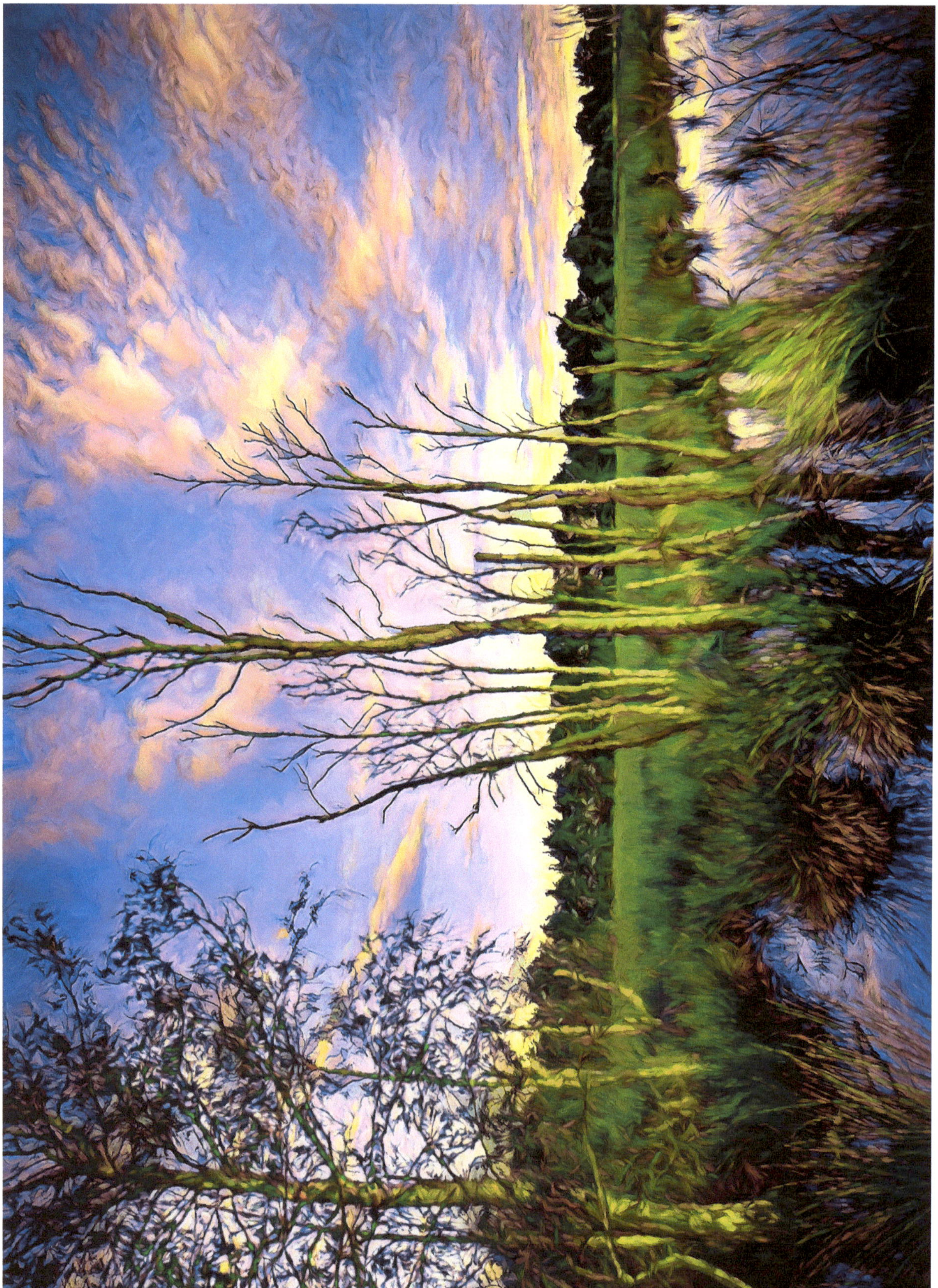

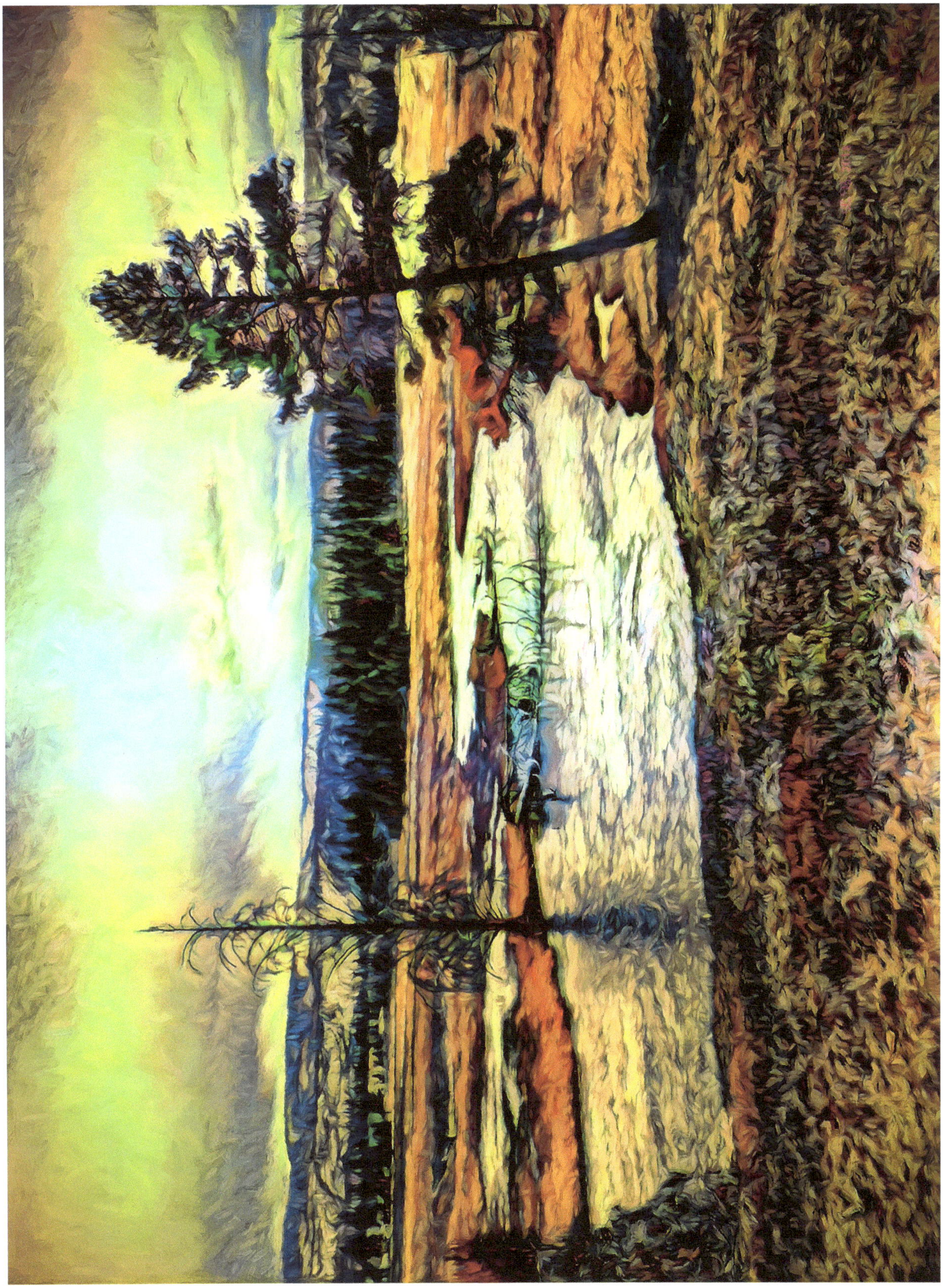

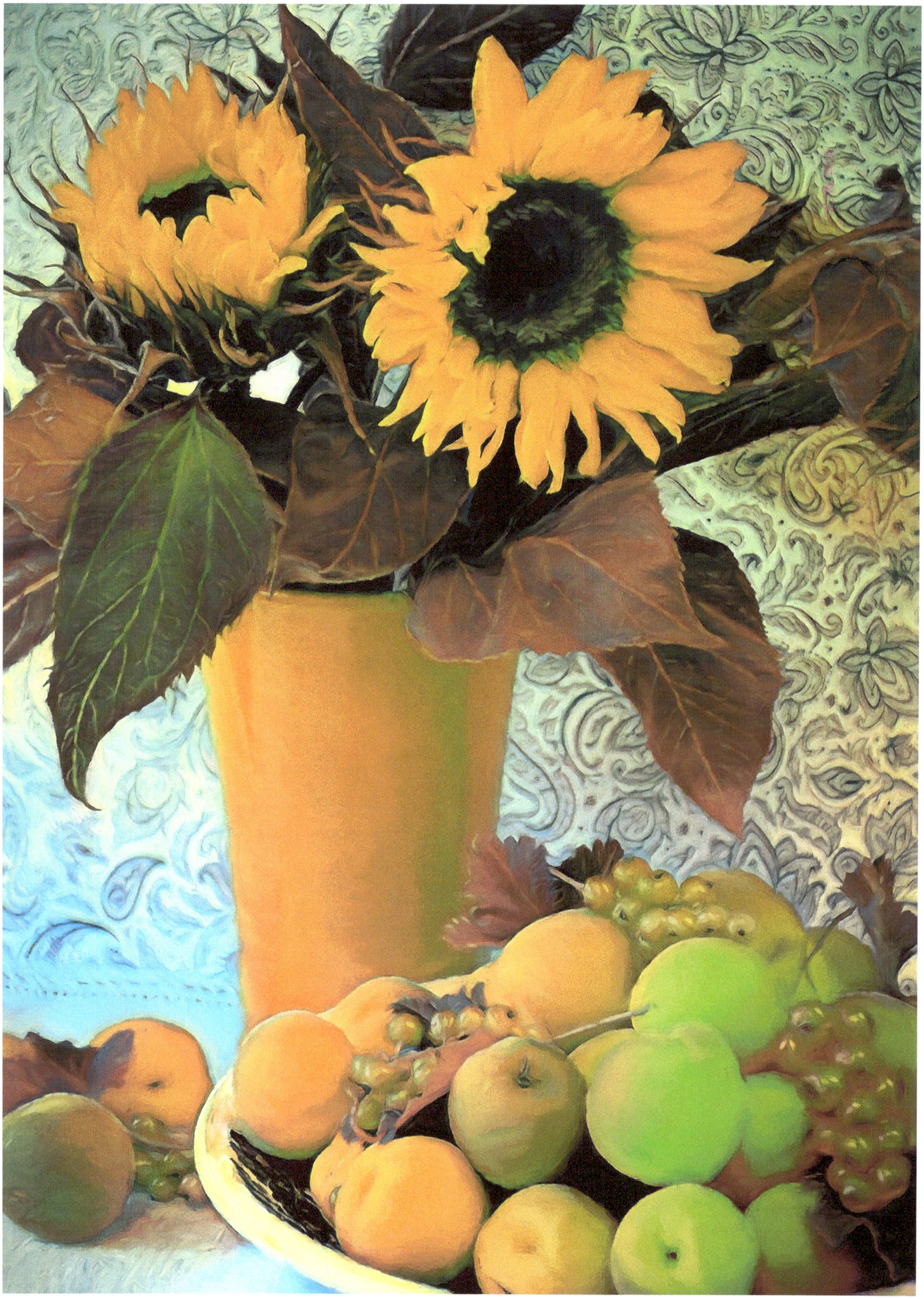

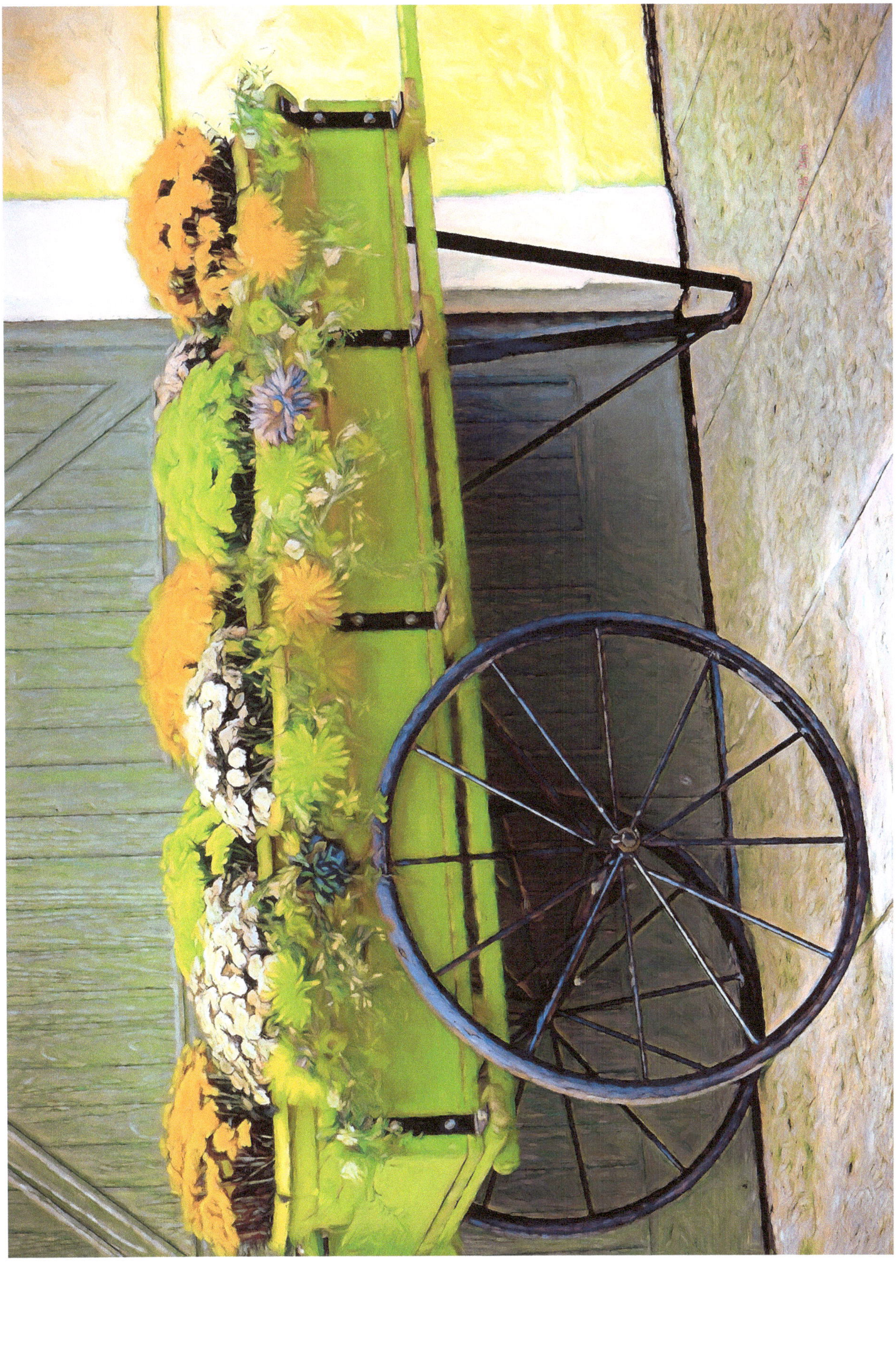

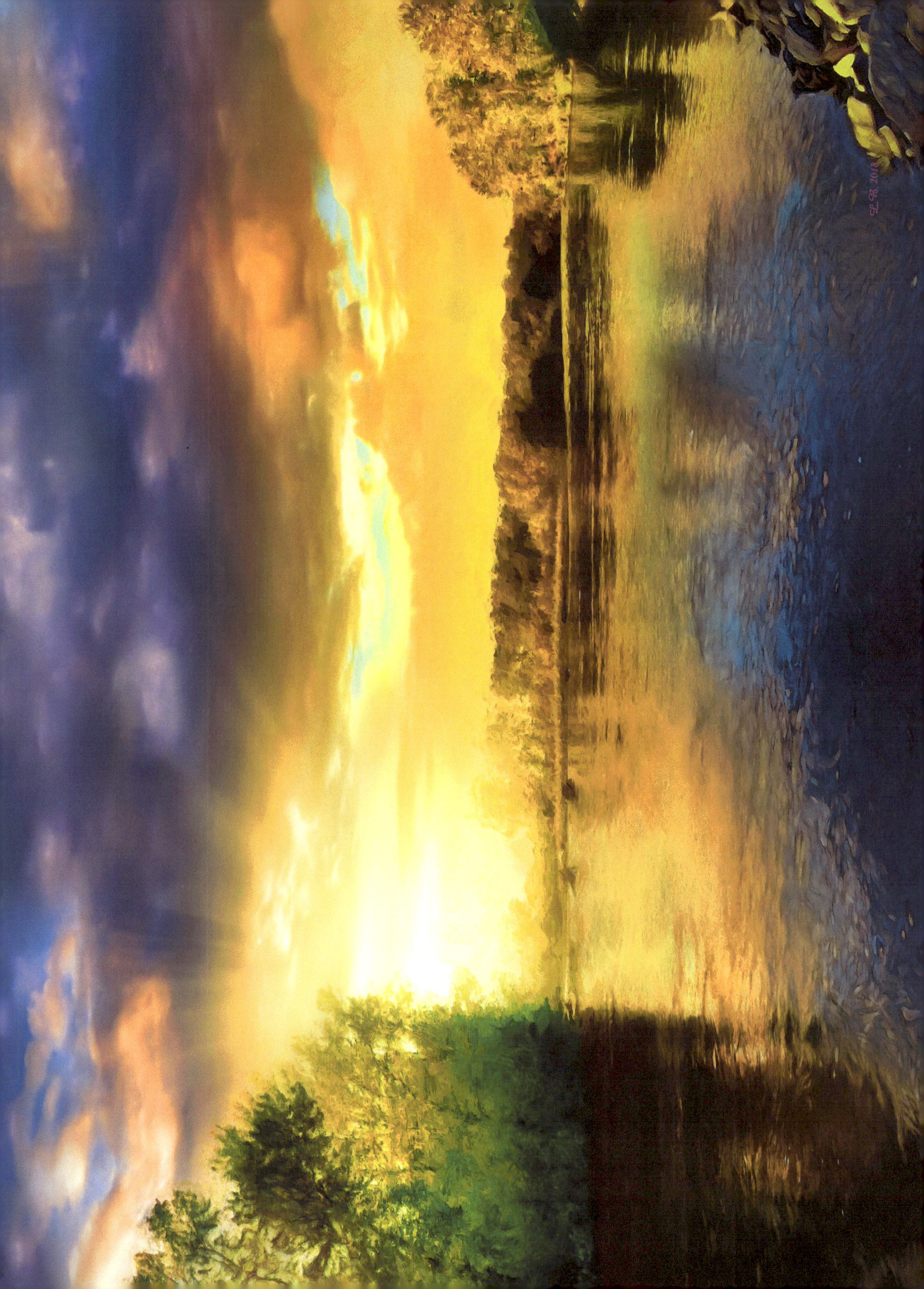

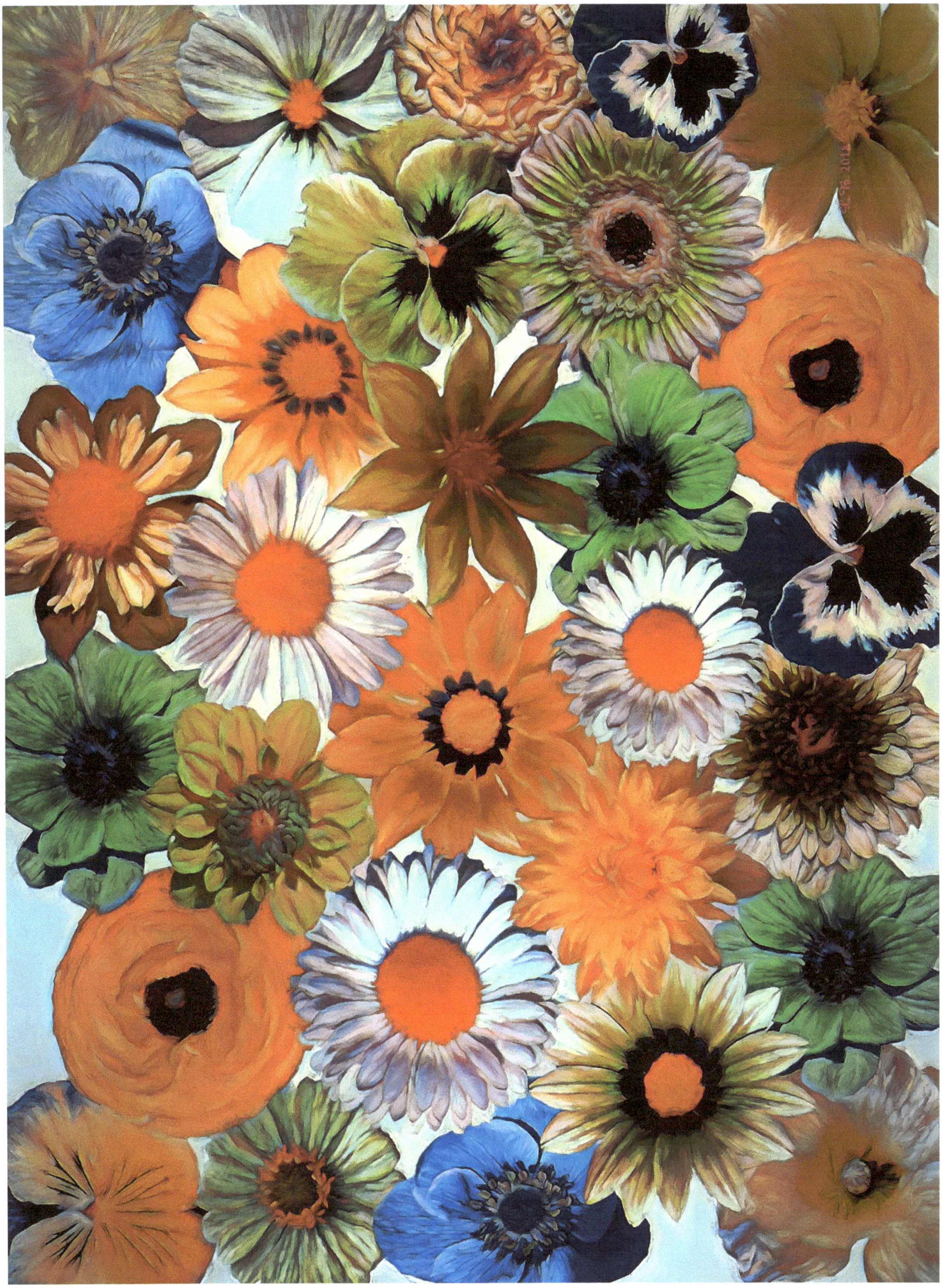

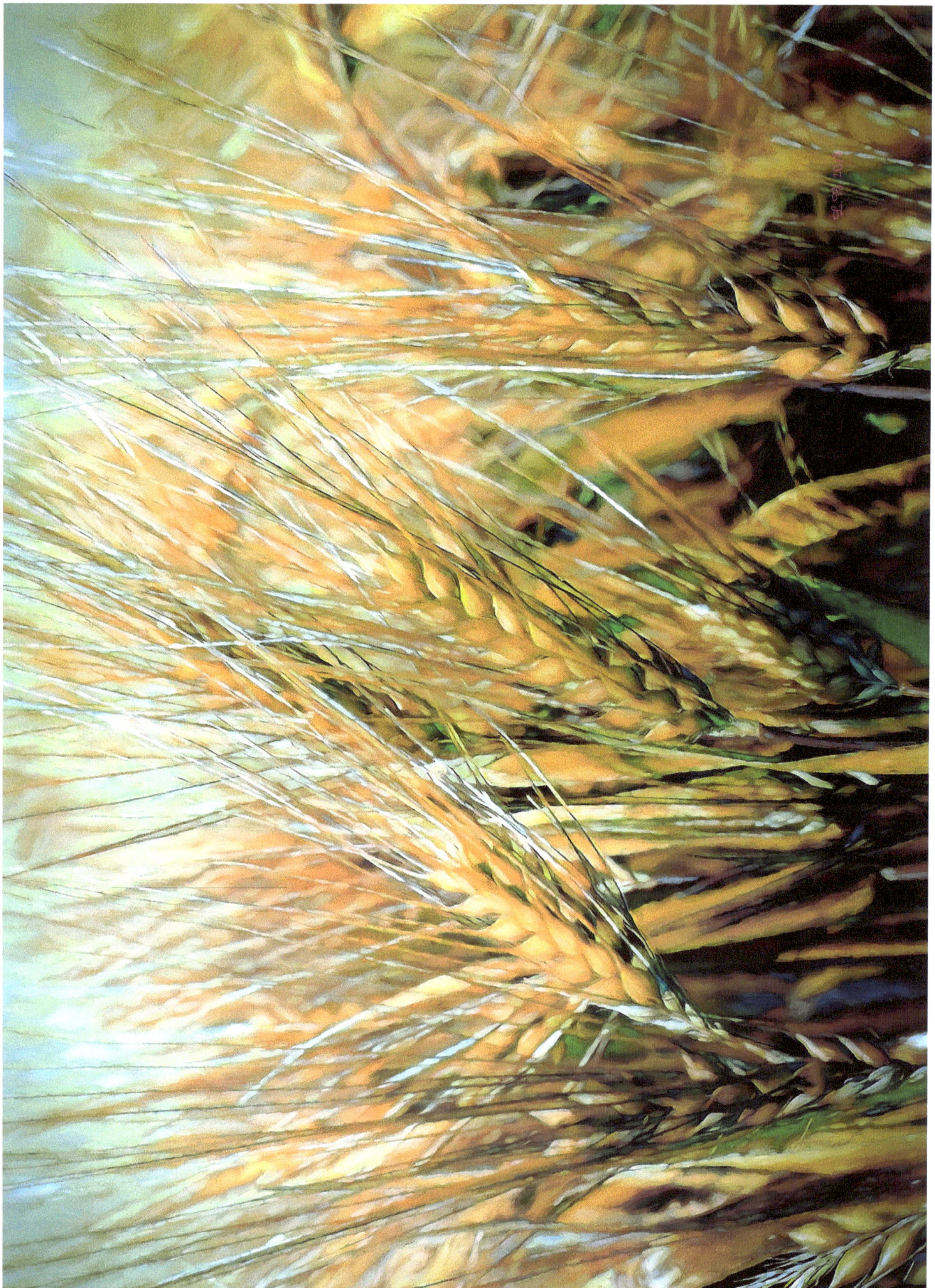

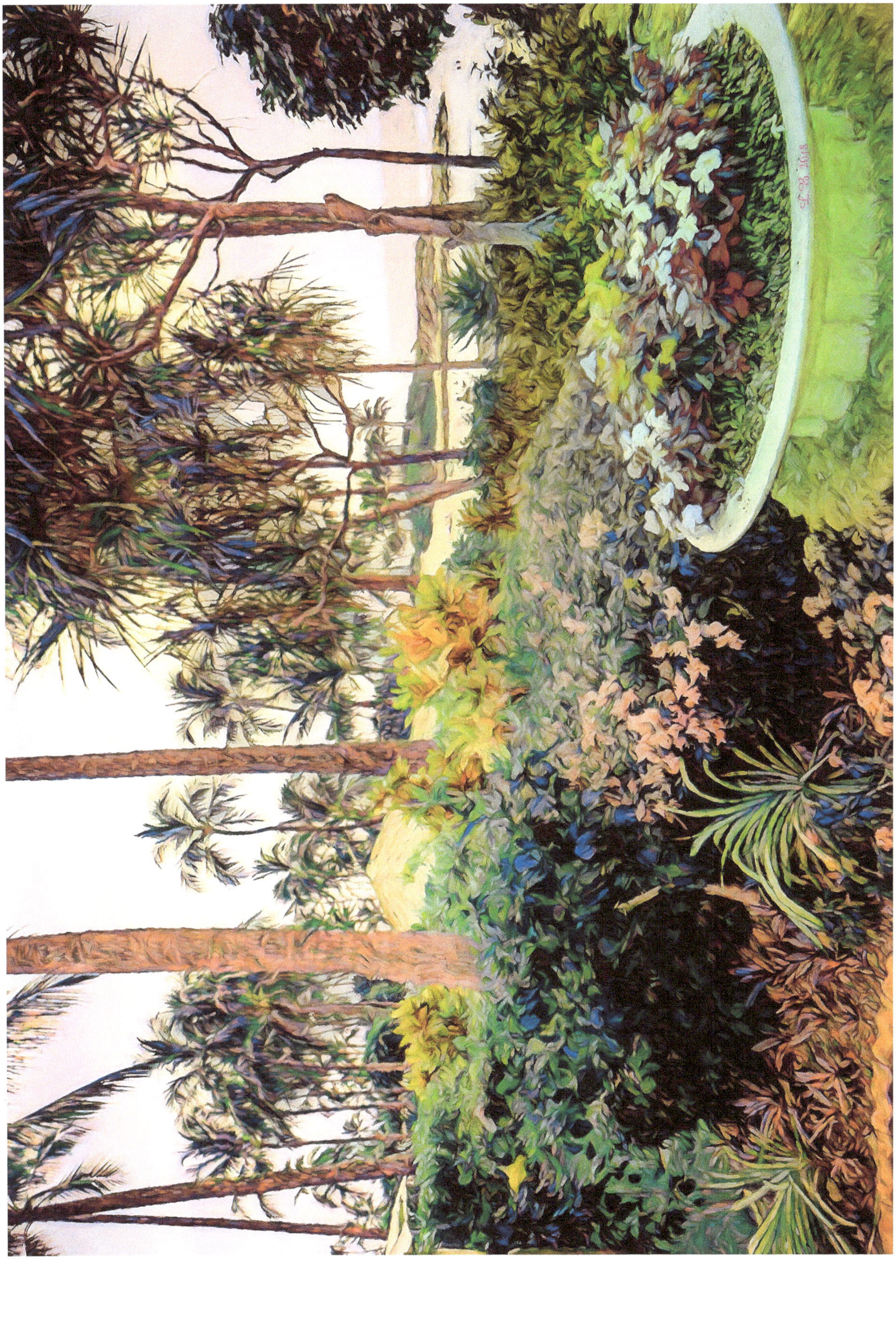

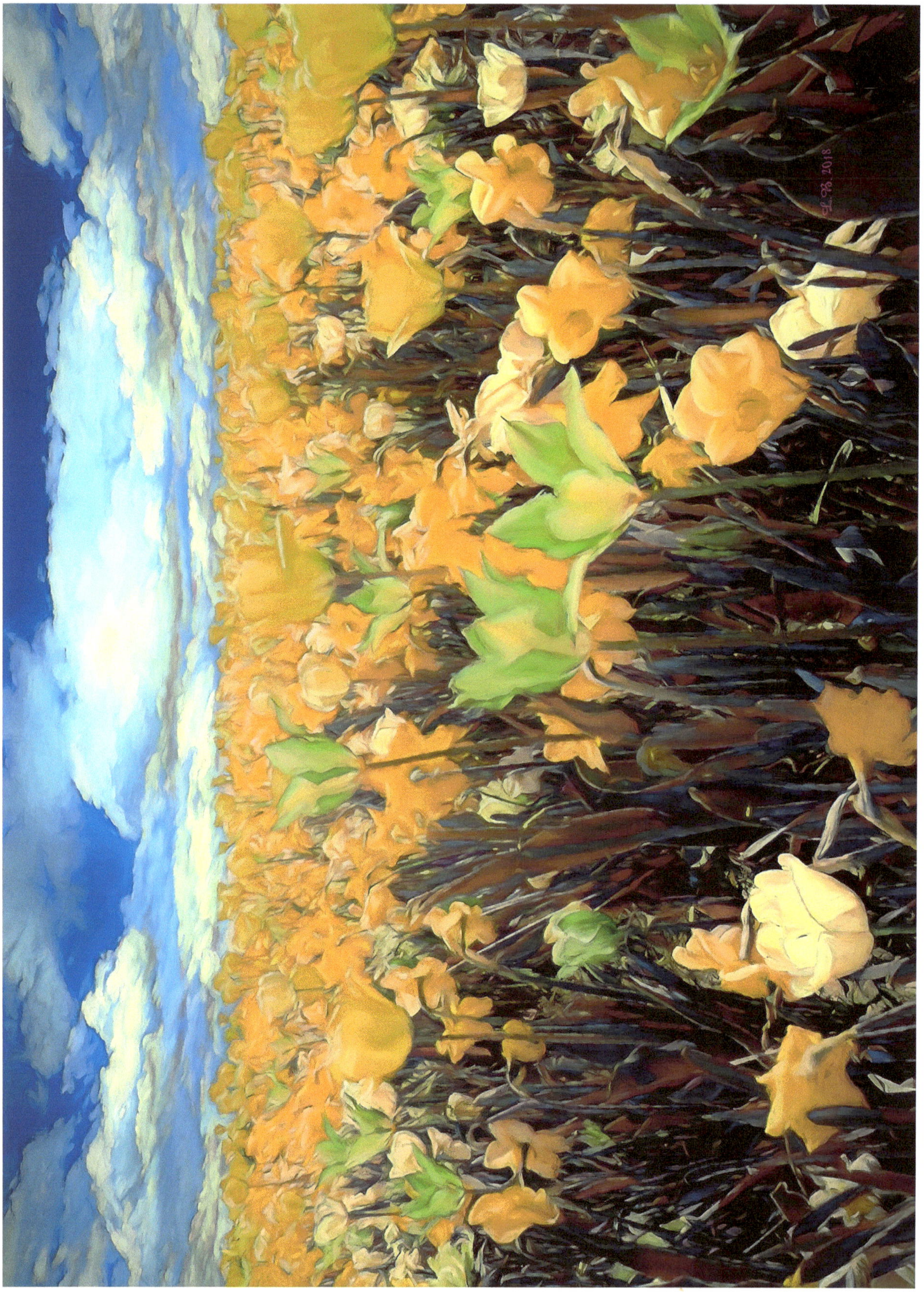

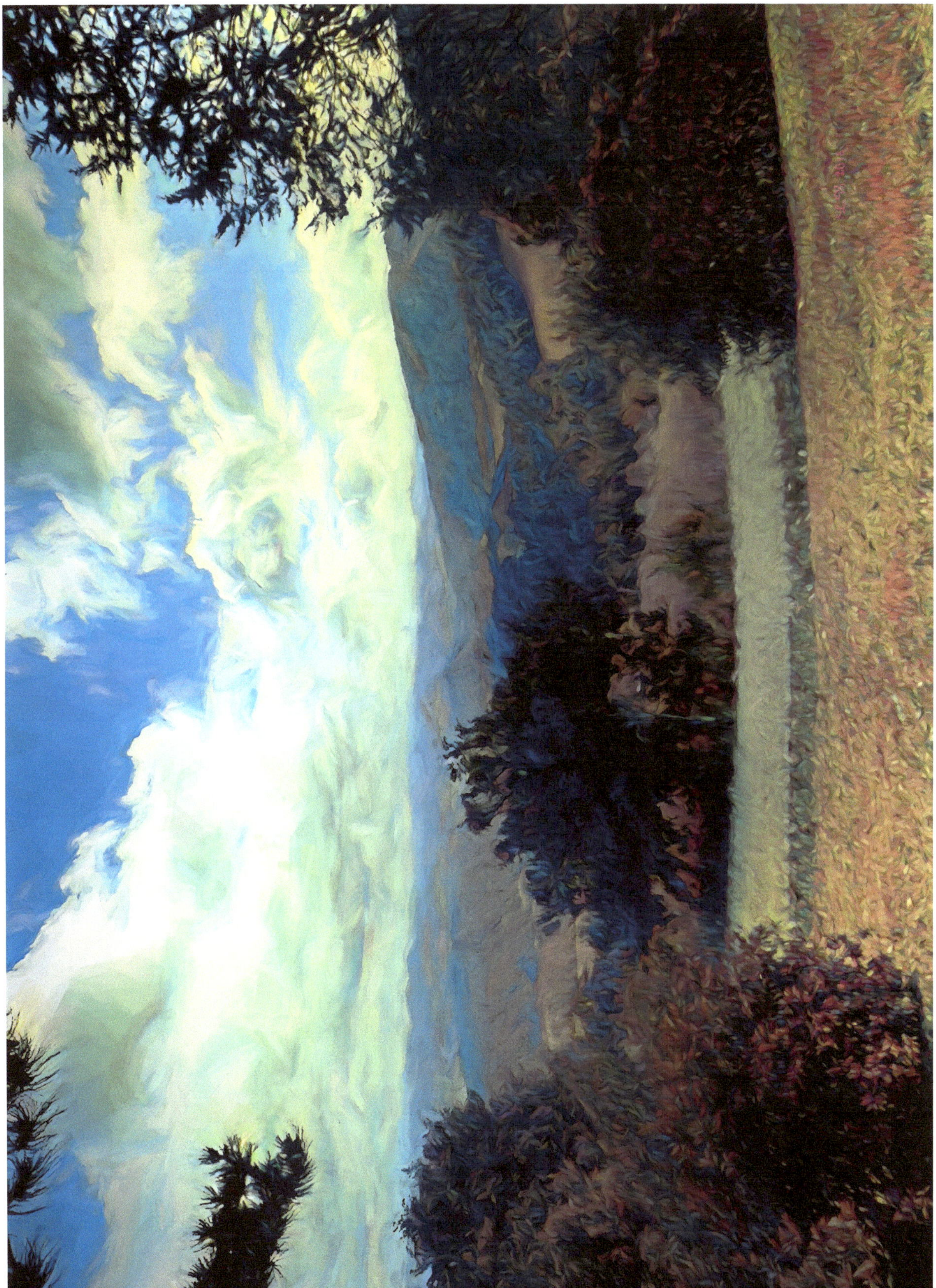

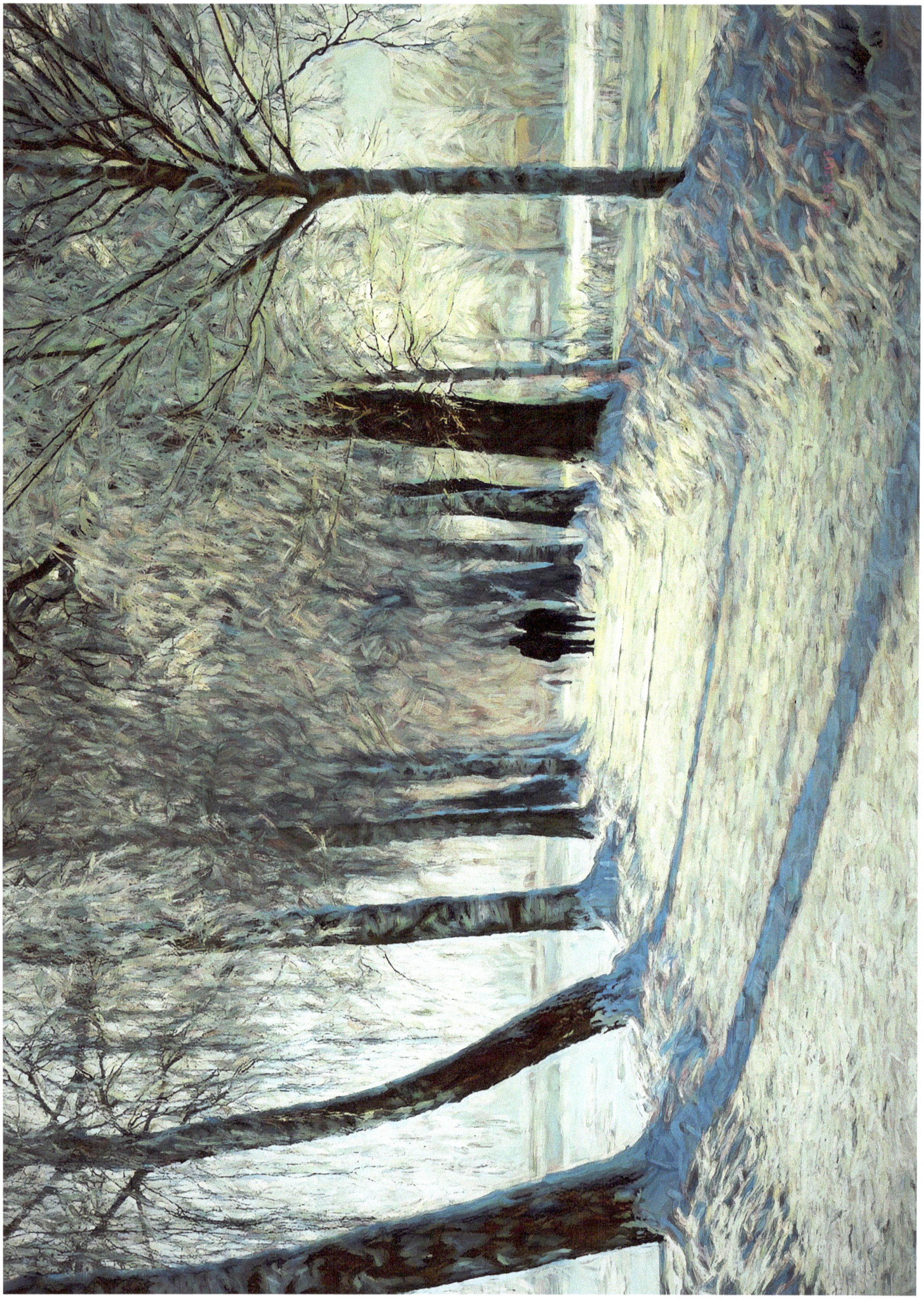

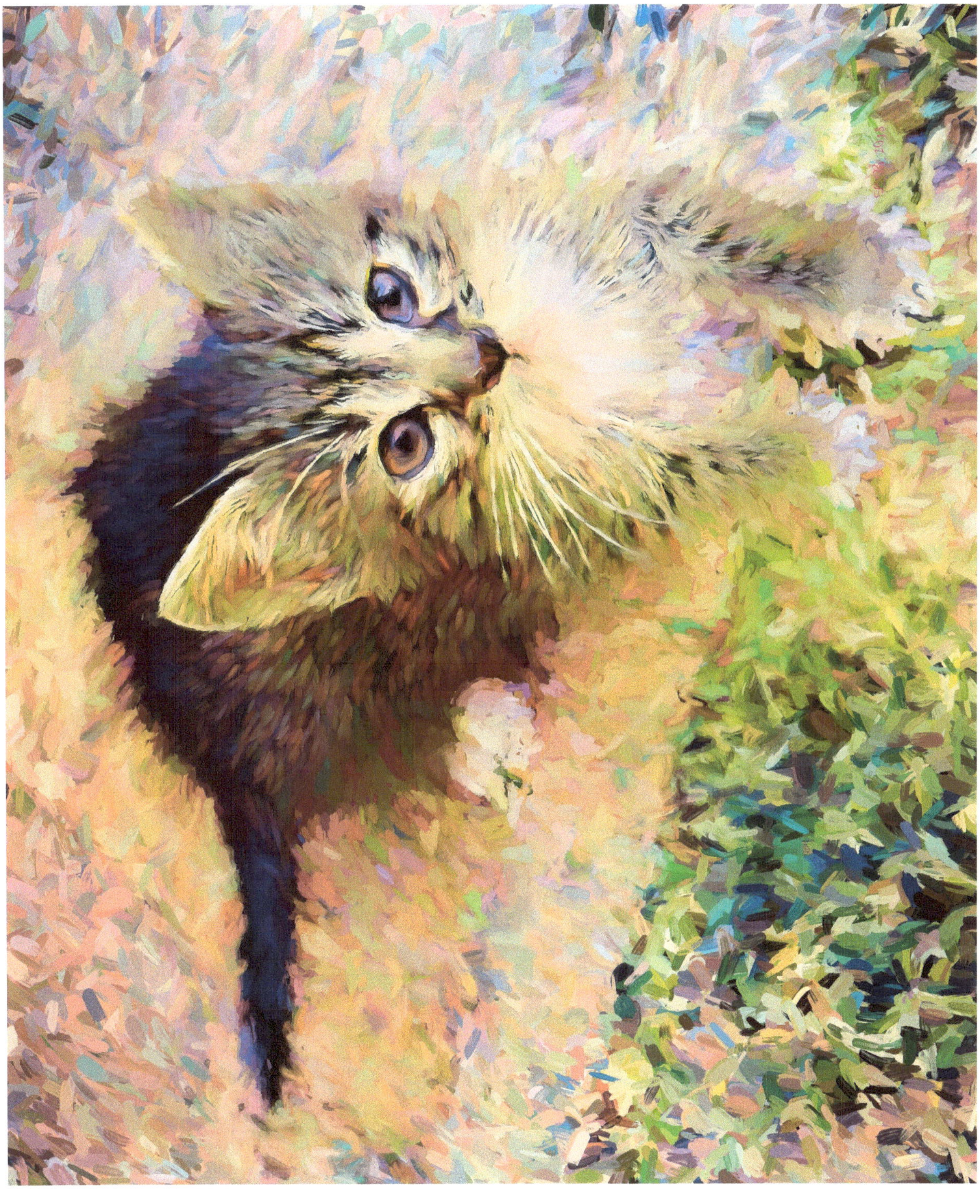

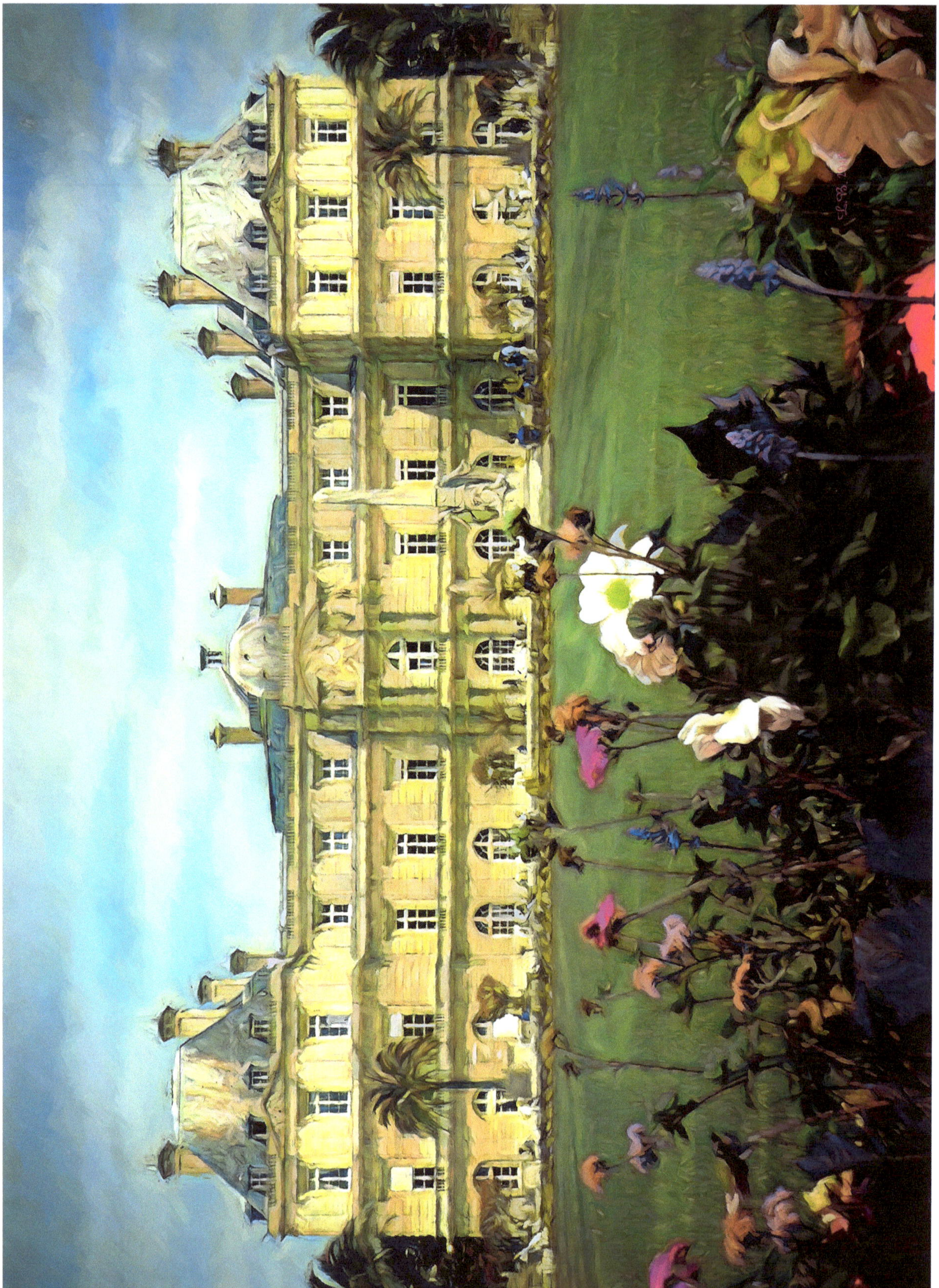

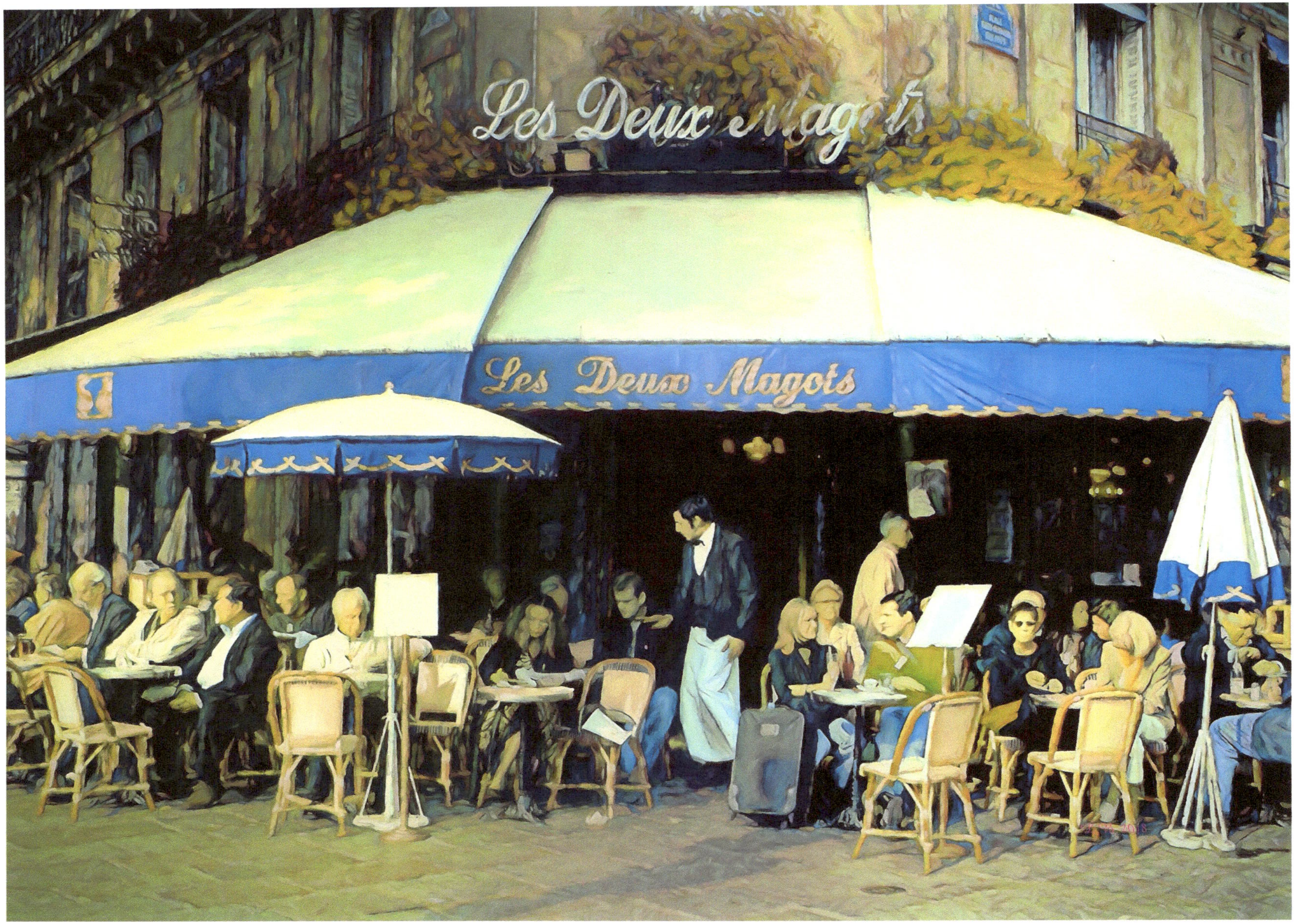
Les Deux Magots
Les Deux Magots

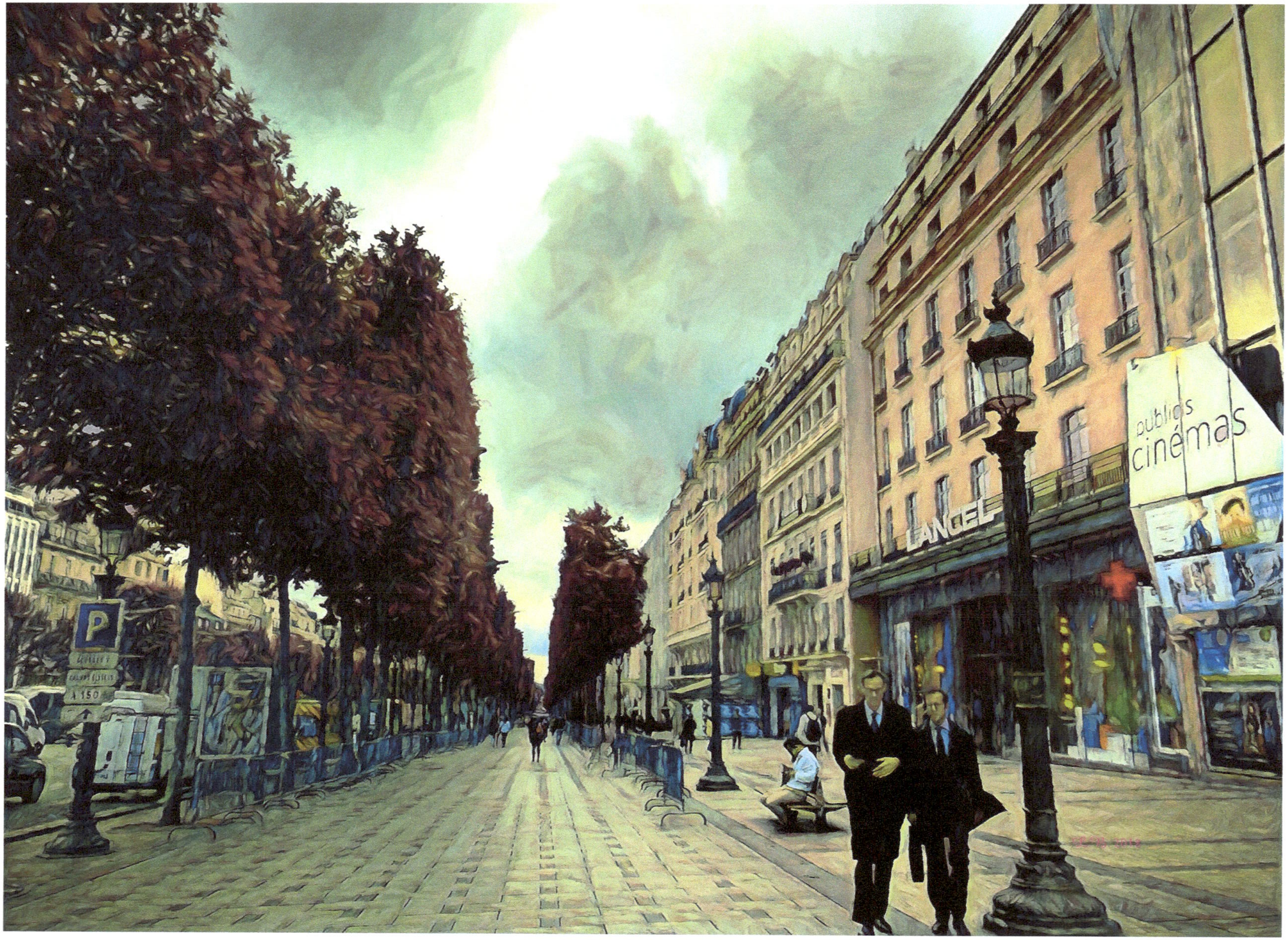
publicis
cinémas
LANCEL
P
A 150

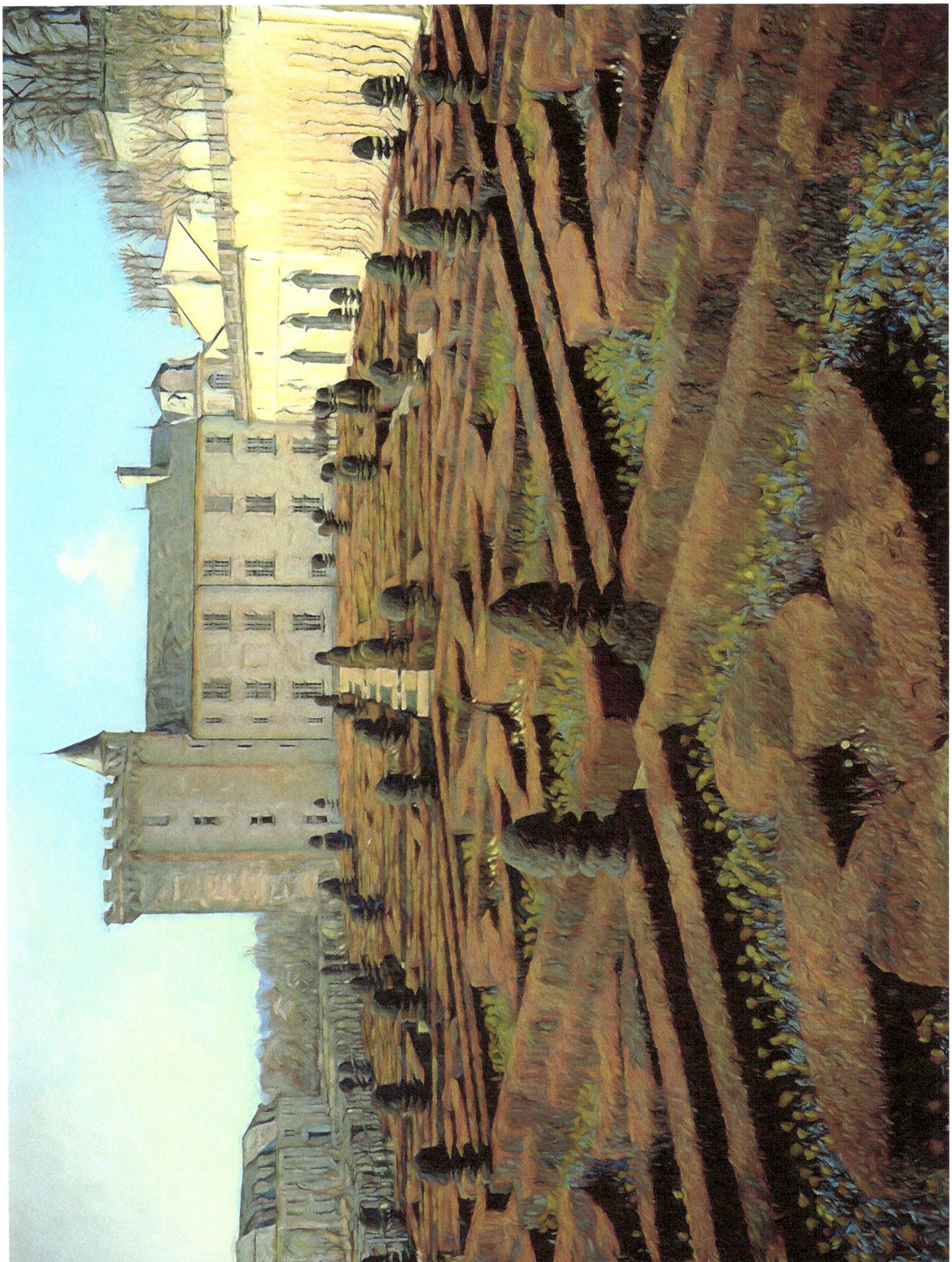

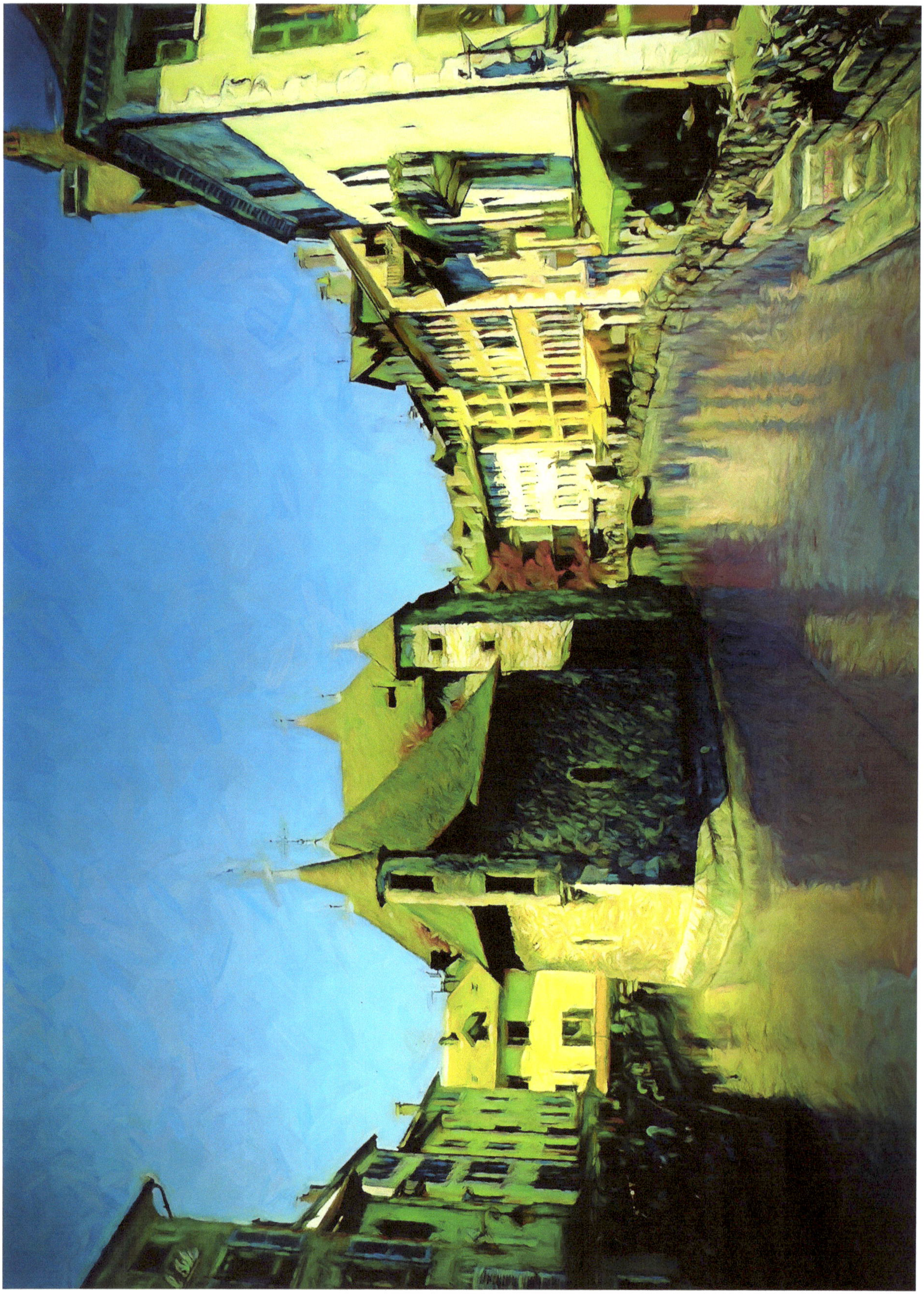

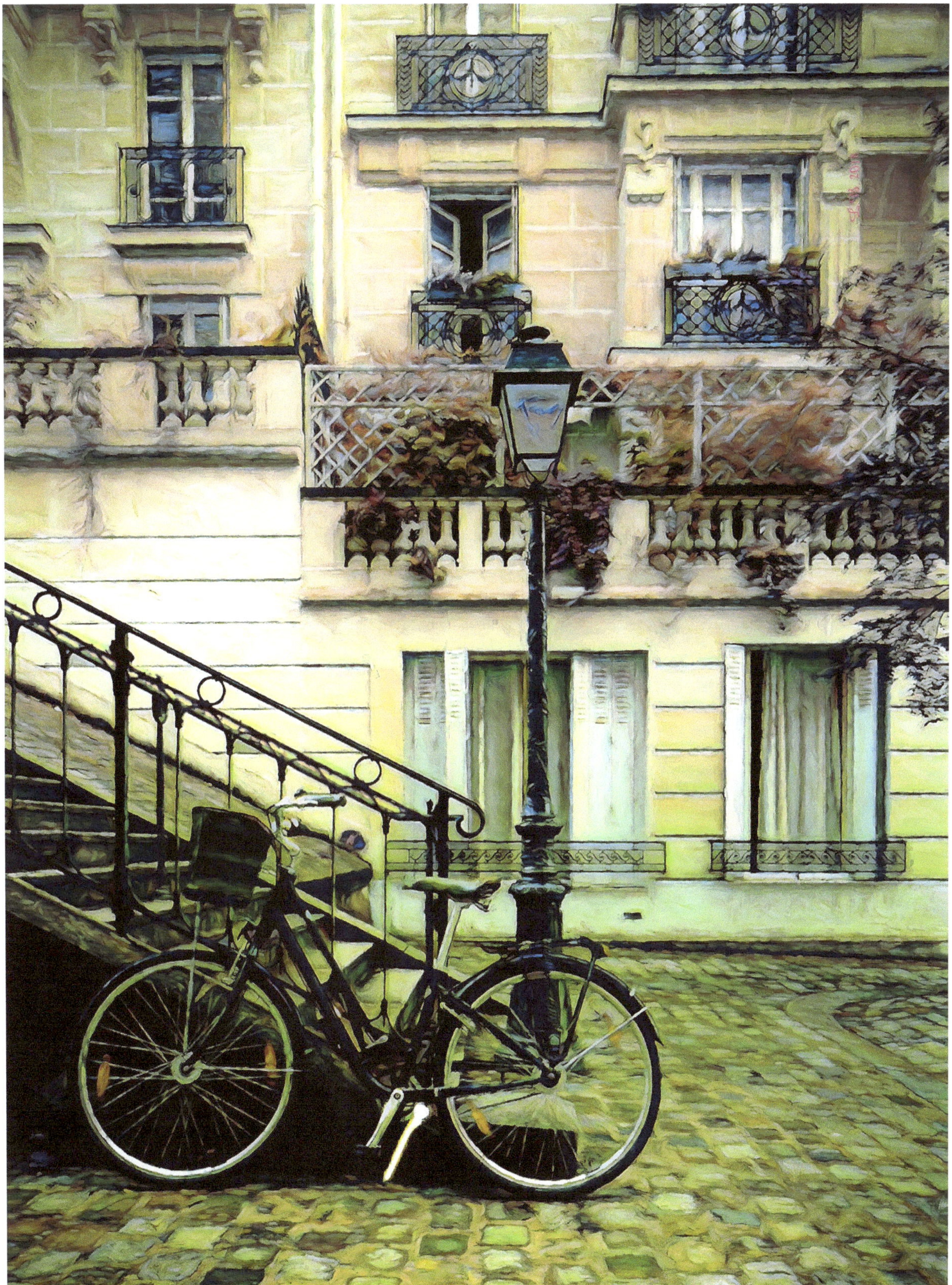

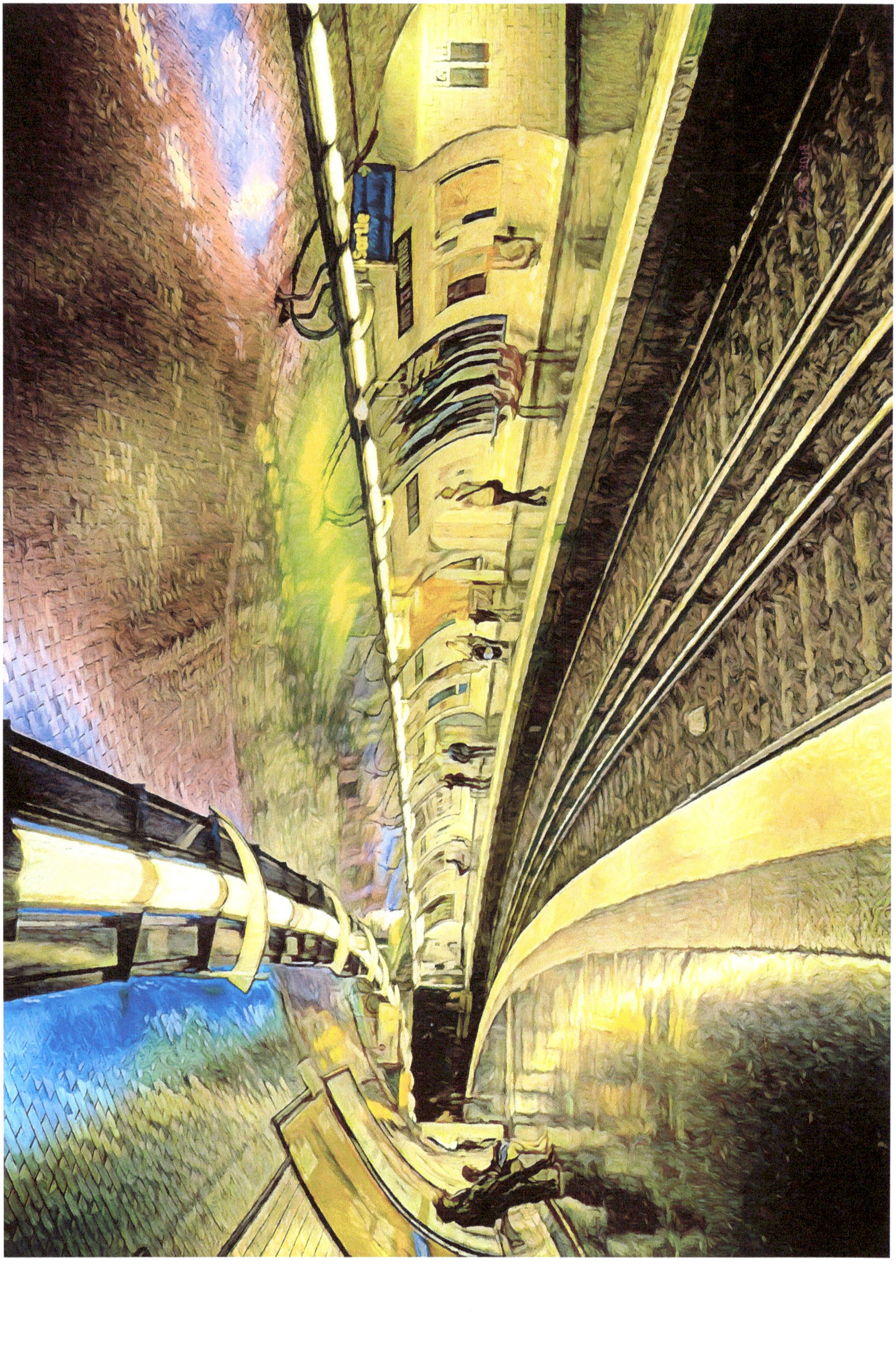
Sortie

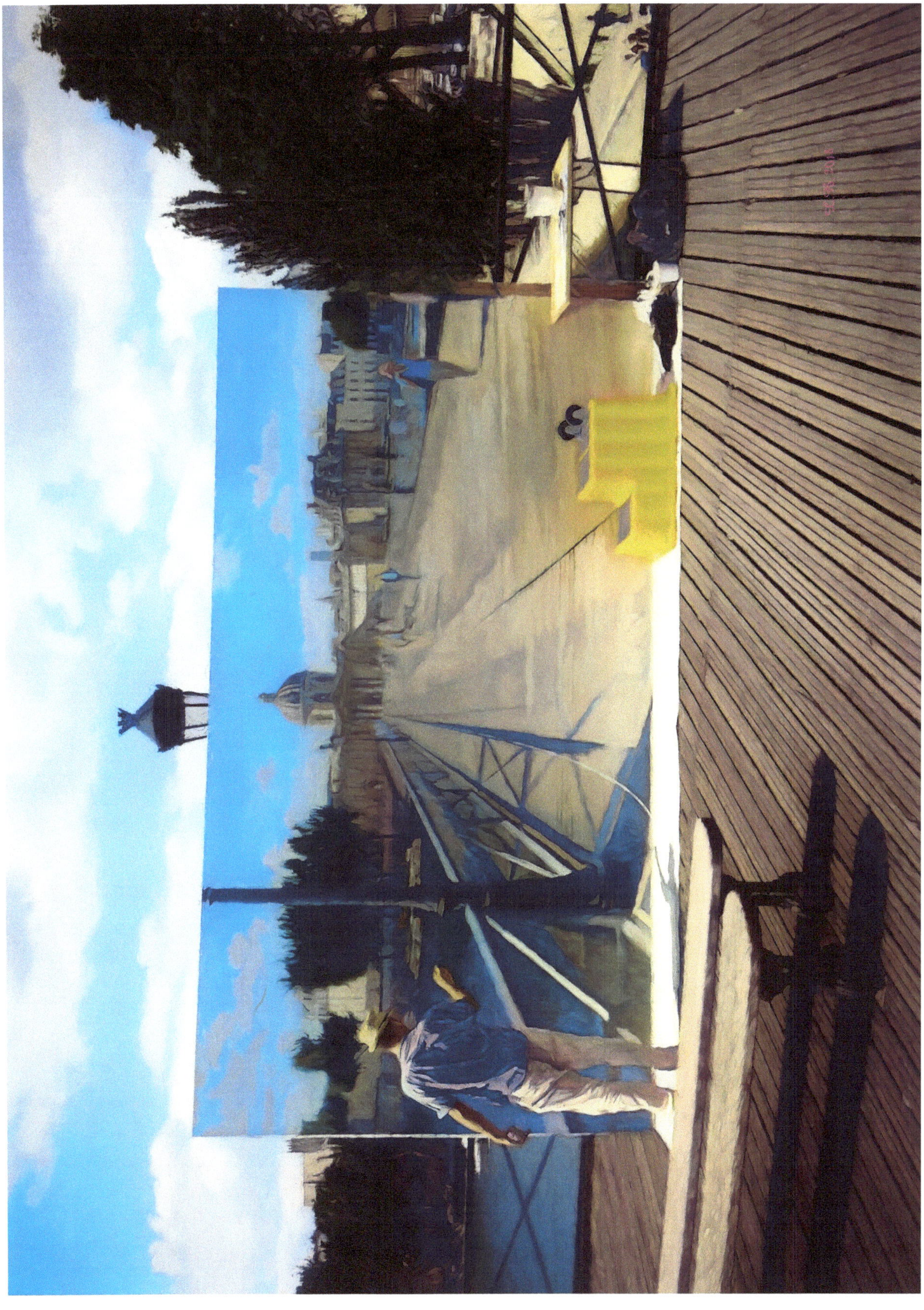

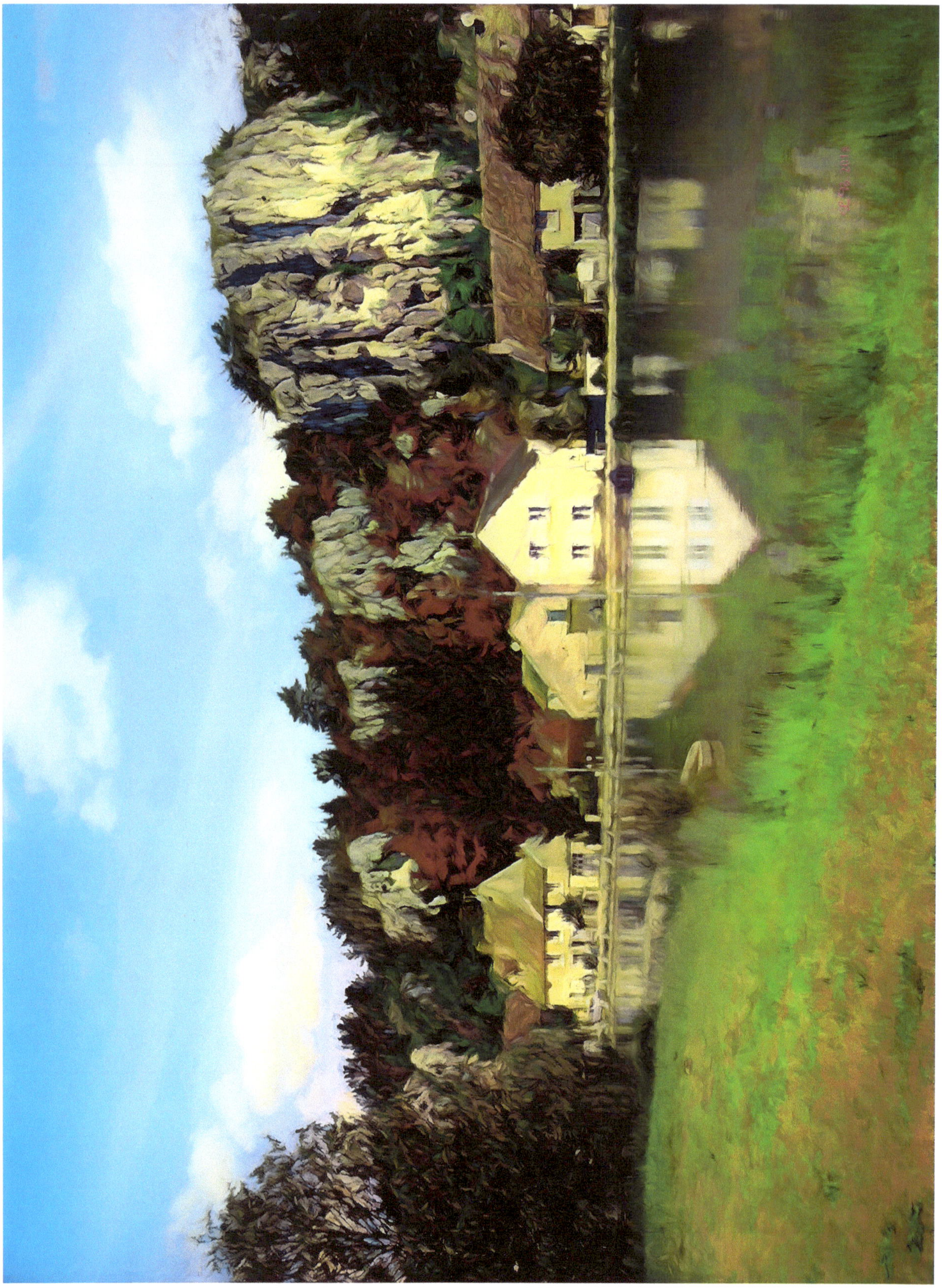

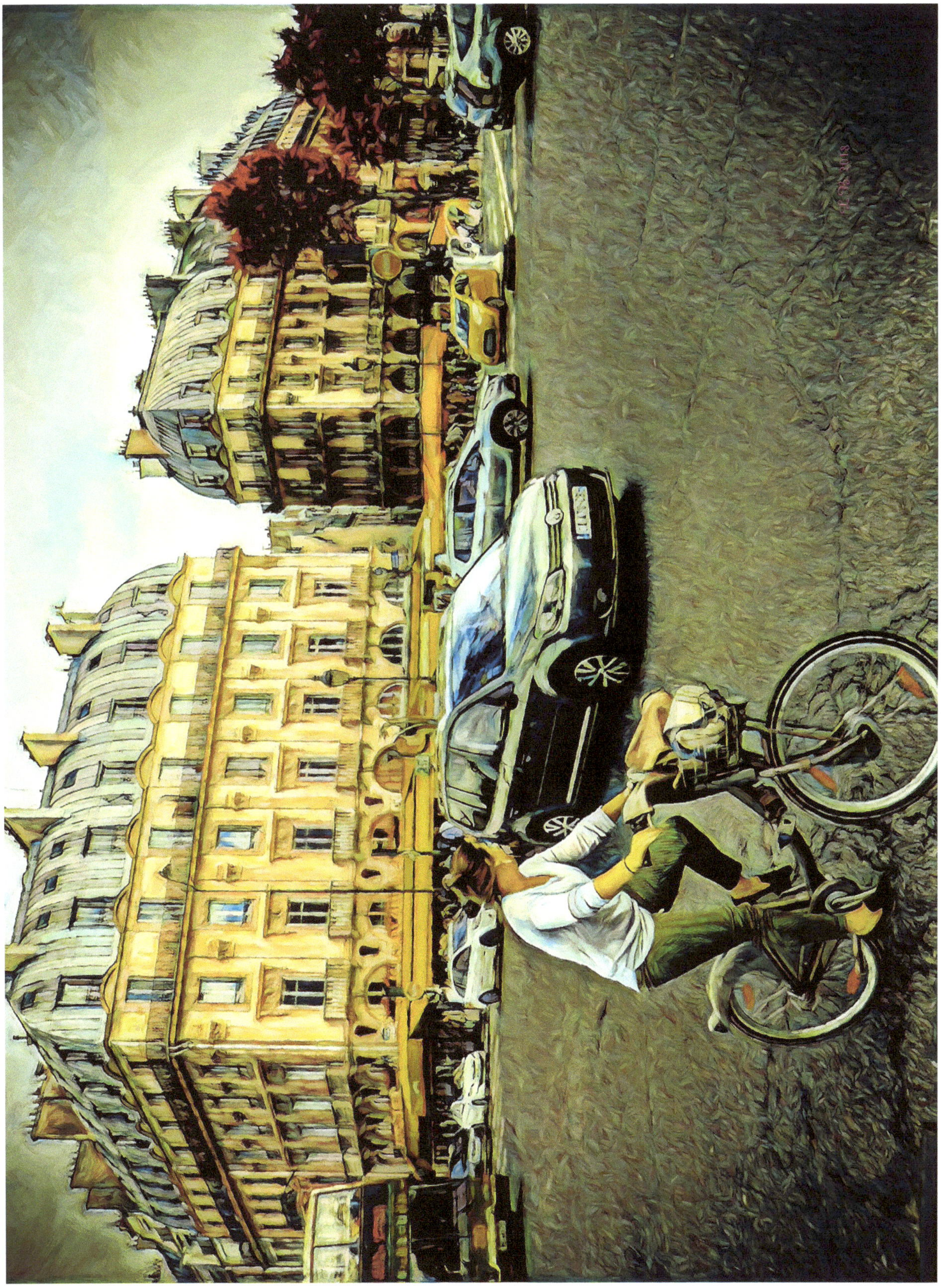

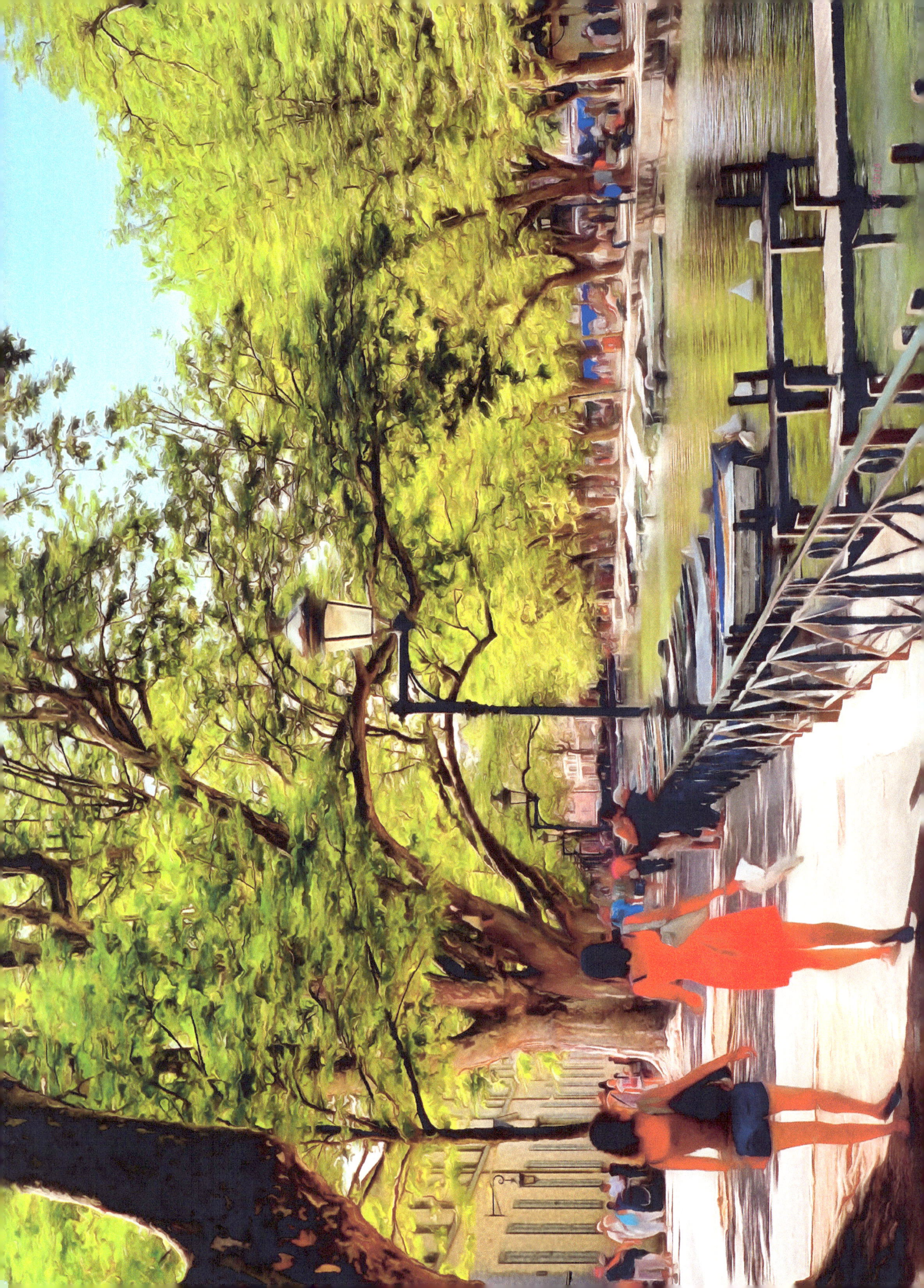

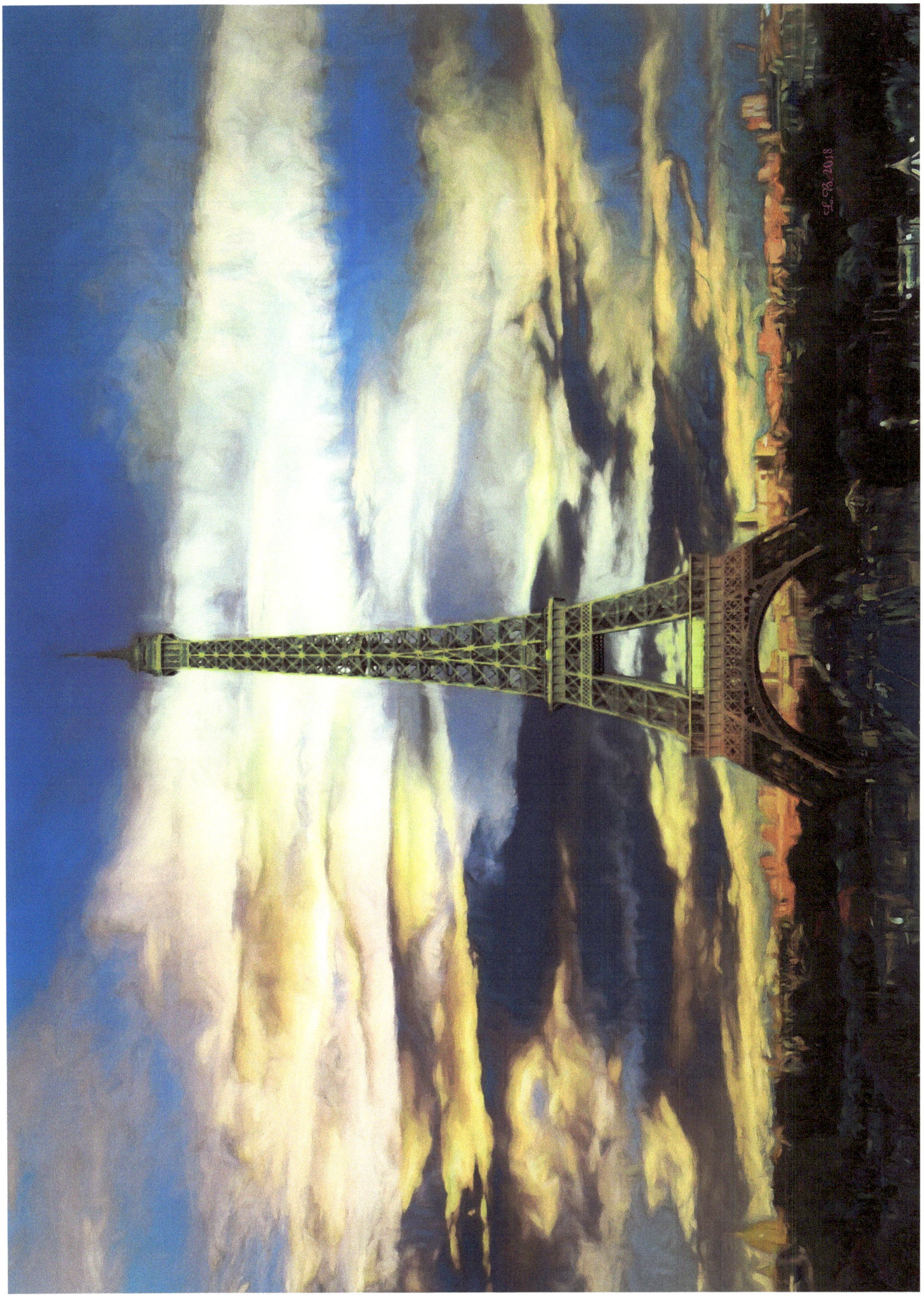

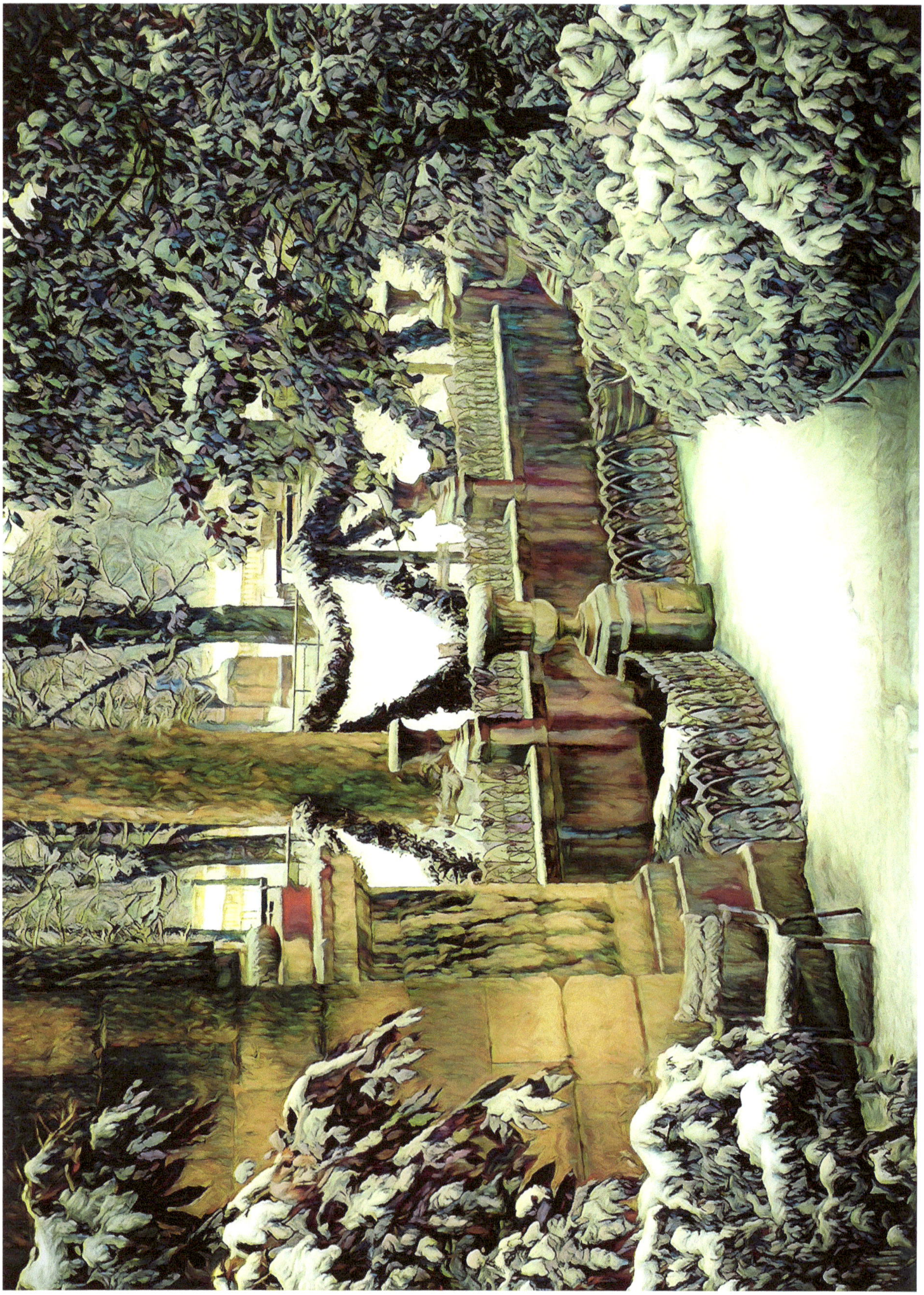

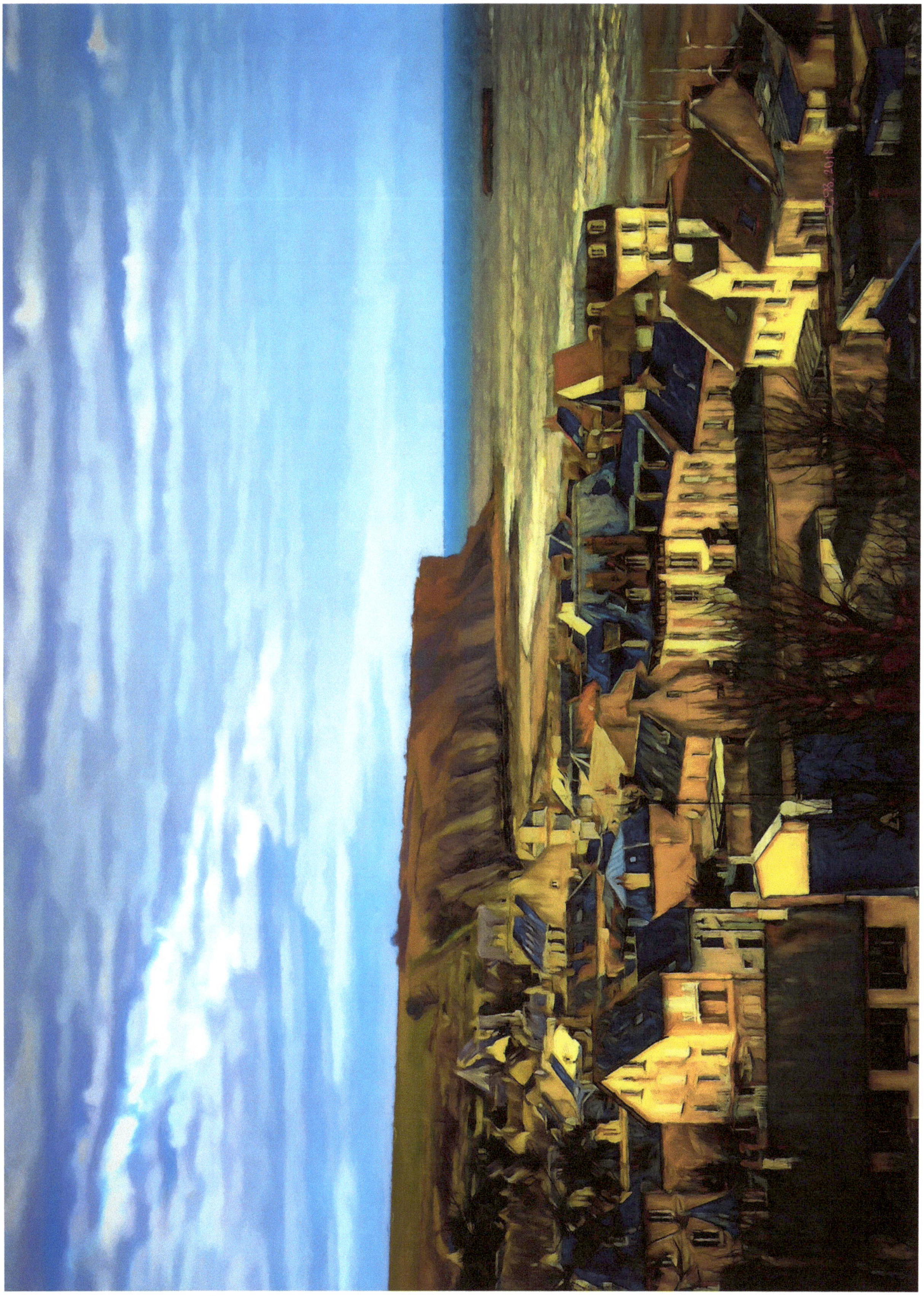

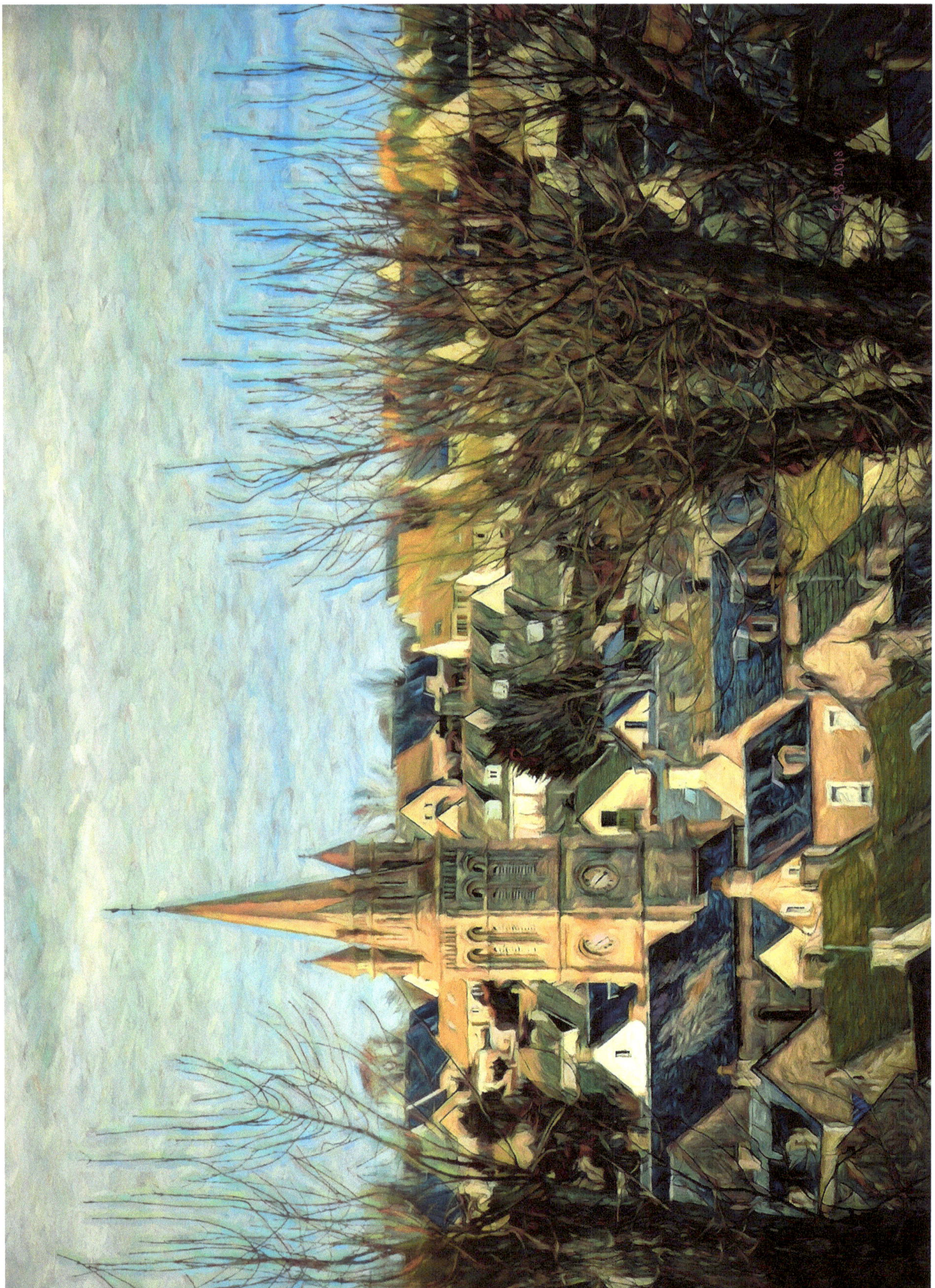

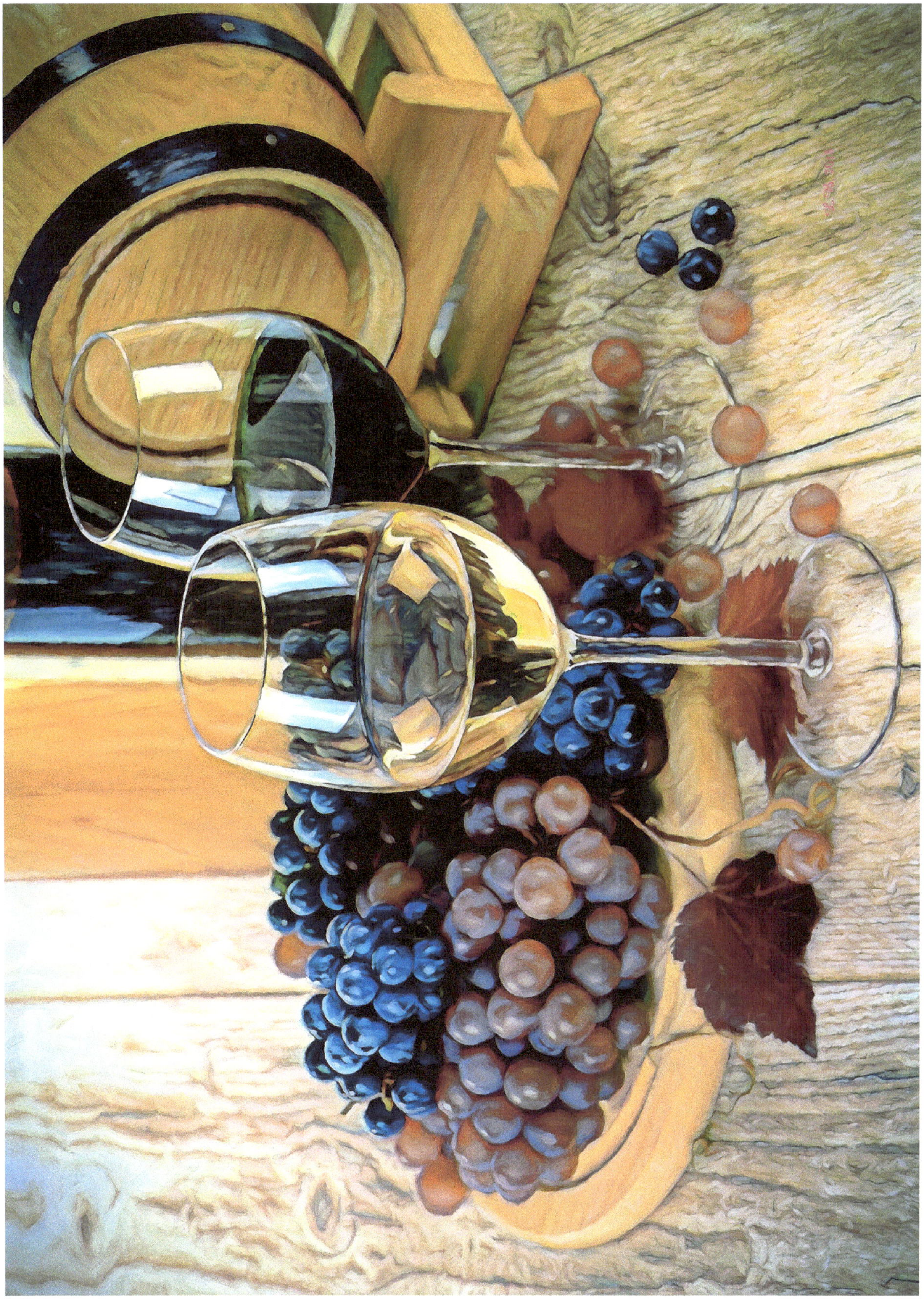

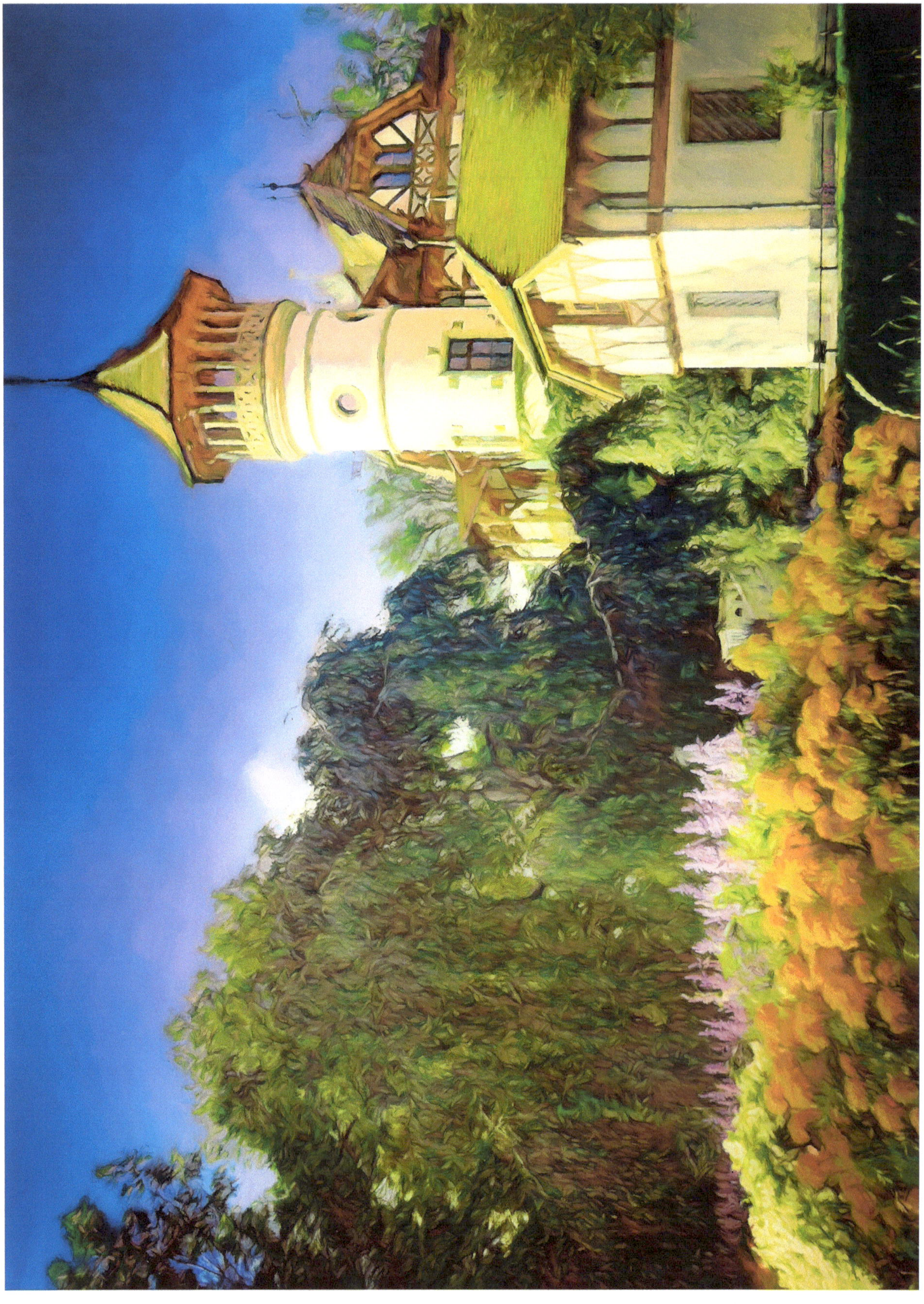

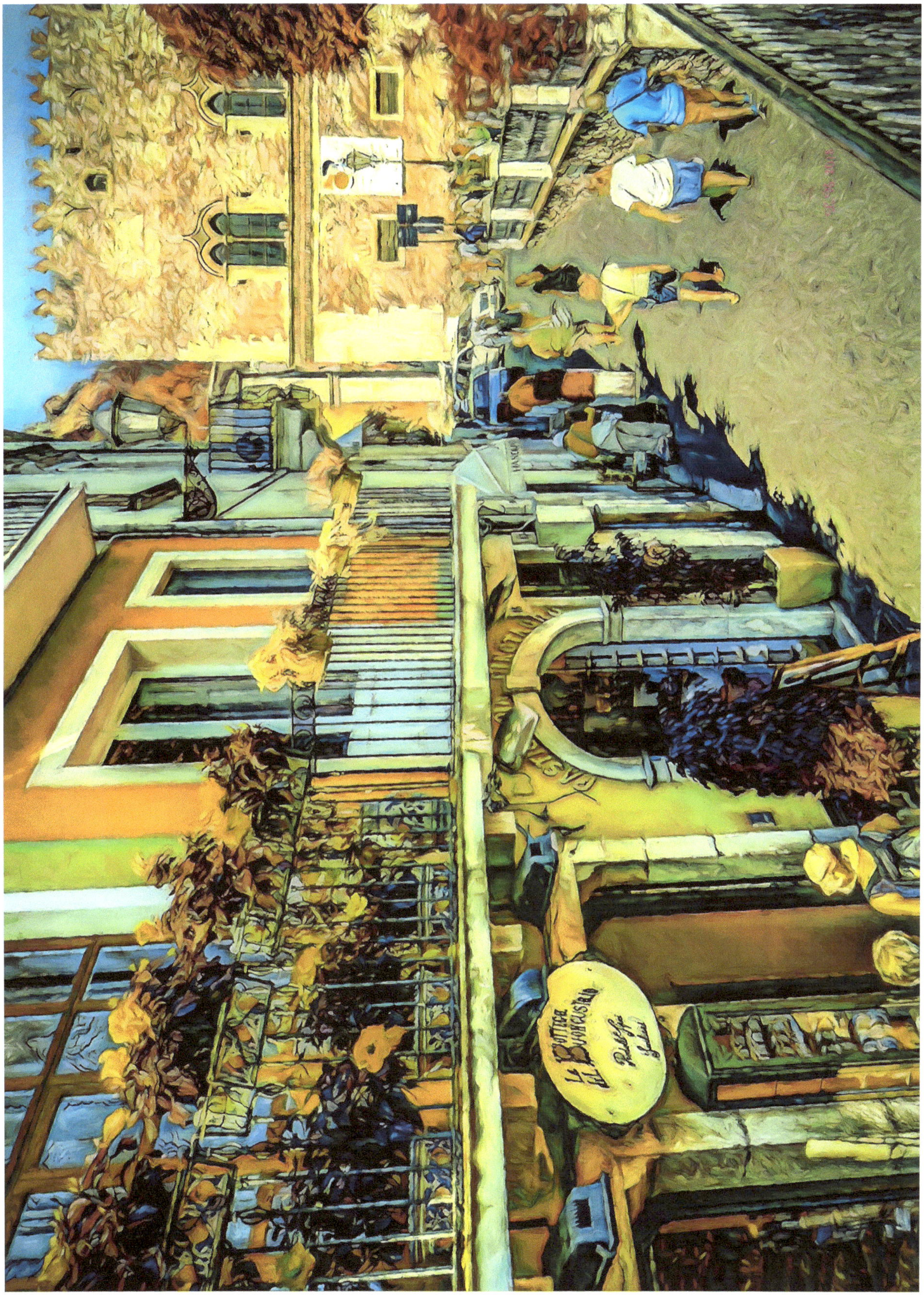

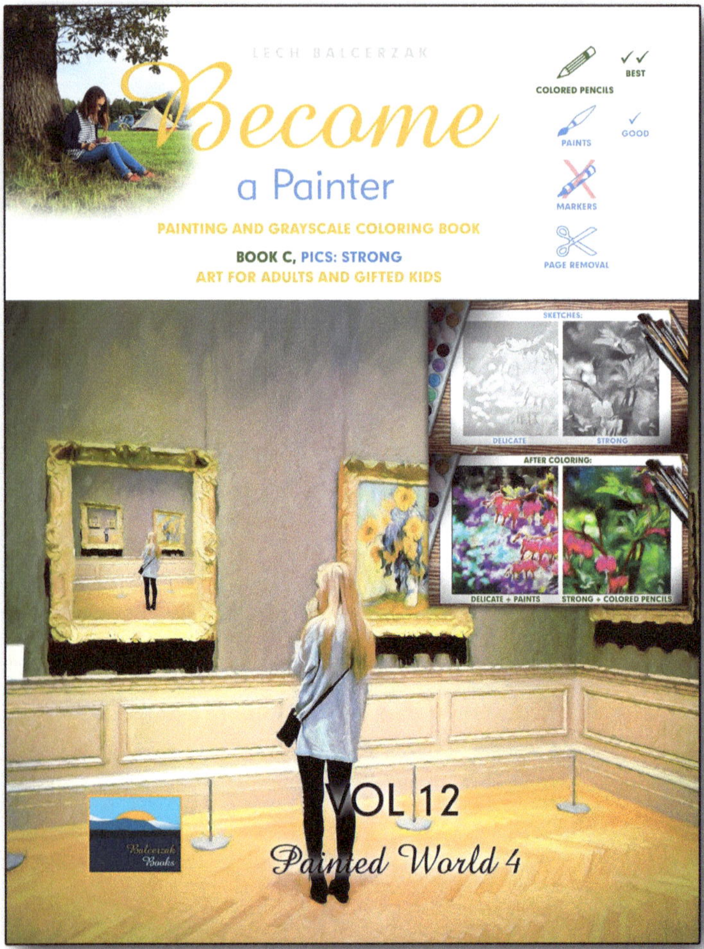
LECH BALCERZAK
Become
a Painter
PAINTING AND GRAYSCALE COLORING BOOK
BOOK C, PICS: STRONG
ART FOR ADULTS AND GIFTED KIDS
COLORED PENCILS
BEST
PAINTS
GOOD
MARKERS
PAGE REMOVAL
SKETCHES:
DELICATE
STRONG
AFTER COLORING:
DELICATE + PAINTS
STRONG + COLORED PENCILS
VOL 12
Painted World 4
Balcerzak Books

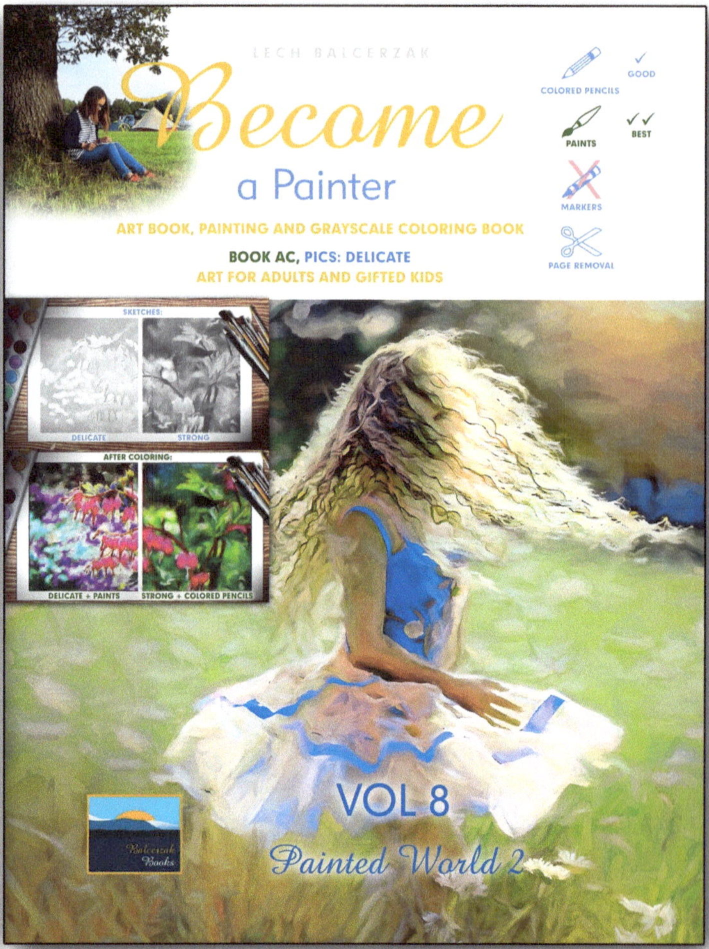
LECH BALCERZAK
Become
a Painter
ART BOOK, PAINTING AND GRAYSCALE COLORING BOOK
BOOK AC, PICS: DELICATE
ART FOR ADULTS AND GIFTED KIDS
COLORED PENCILS
GOOD
PAINTS
BEST
MARKERS
PAGE REMOVAL
SKETCHES:
DELICATE
STRONG
AFTER COLORING:
DELICATE + PAINTS
STRONG + COLORED PENCILS
VOL 8
Painted World 2
Balcerzak Books

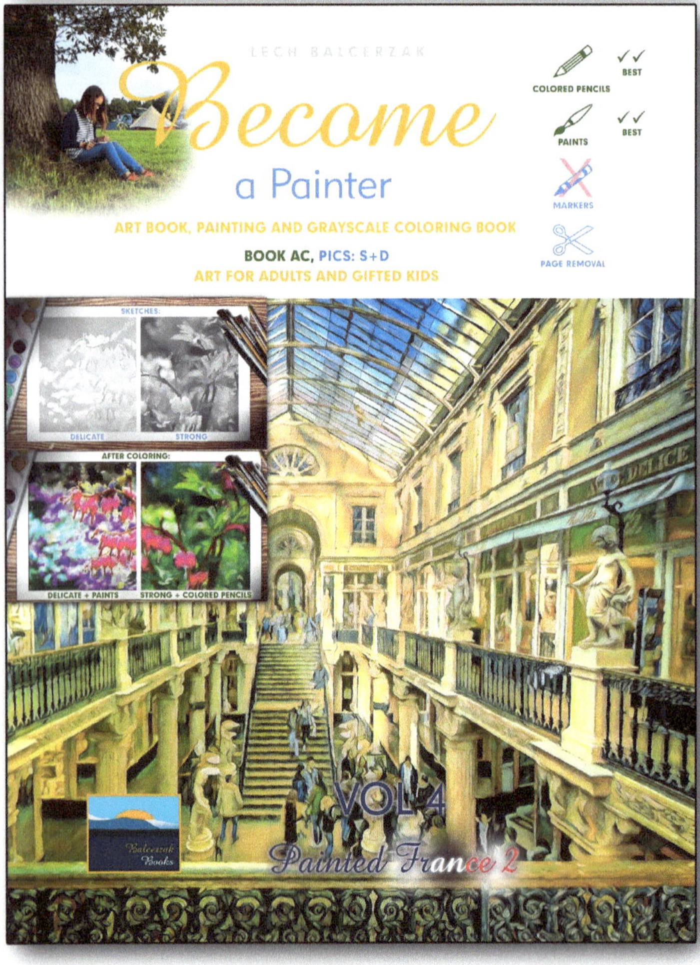
LECH BALCERZAK
Become
a Painter
ART BOOK, PAINTING AND GRAYSCALE COLORING BOOK
BOOK AC, PICS: S+D
ART FOR ADULTS AND GIFTED KIDS
COLORED PENCILS
BEST
PAINTS
BEST
MARKERS
PAGE REMOVAL
SKETCHES:
DELICATE
STRONG
AFTER COLORING:
DELICATE + PAINTS
STRONG + COLORED PENCILS
VOL 4
Painted France 2
Balcerzak Books

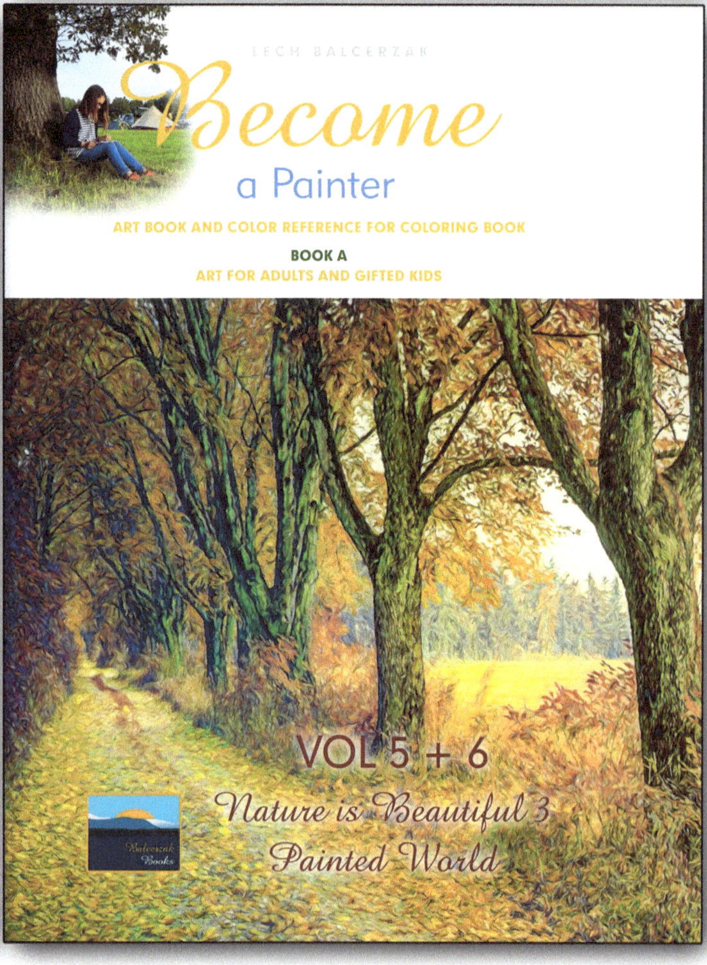
LECH BALCERZAK
Become
a Painter
ART BOOK AND COLOR REFERENCE FOR COLORING BOOK
BOOK A
ART FOR ADULTS AND GIFTED KIDS
VOL 5 + 6
Nature is Beautiful 3
Painted World
Balcerzak Books

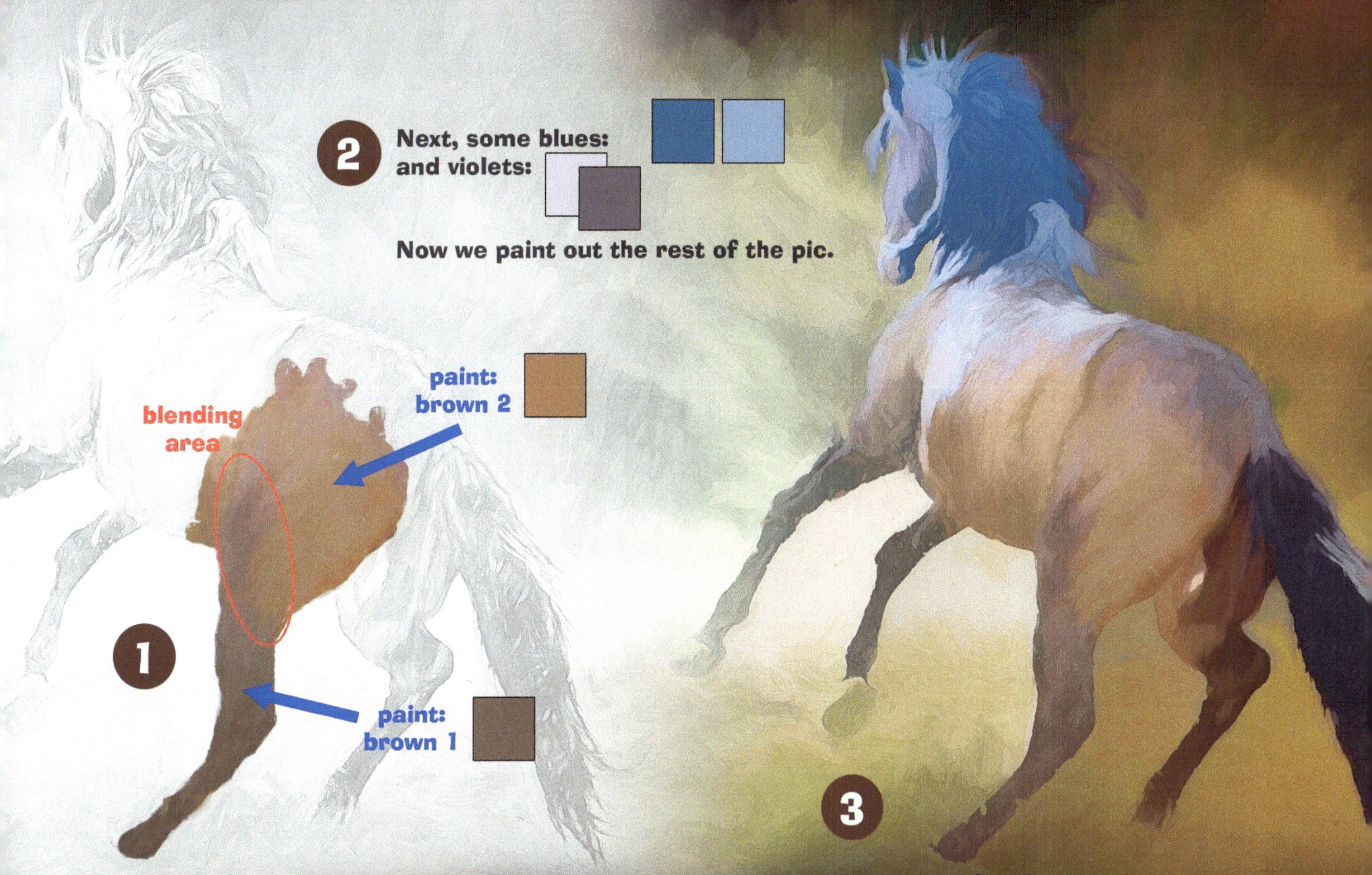

We start with two paints: the brown 1 (more black) and the brown 2 (more yellow)

The raw picture after basic colorization

Mini Guide, example 1

How to Color Delicate Sketches Using Paints?

Painting / coloring is very pleasant and simple - even for your kids - if you use my sketches instead of blank pages. Just choose a color, then follow the shapes and lines and paint, using my color reference pictures (original illustrations printed in color). Or use your own colors (advanced users).

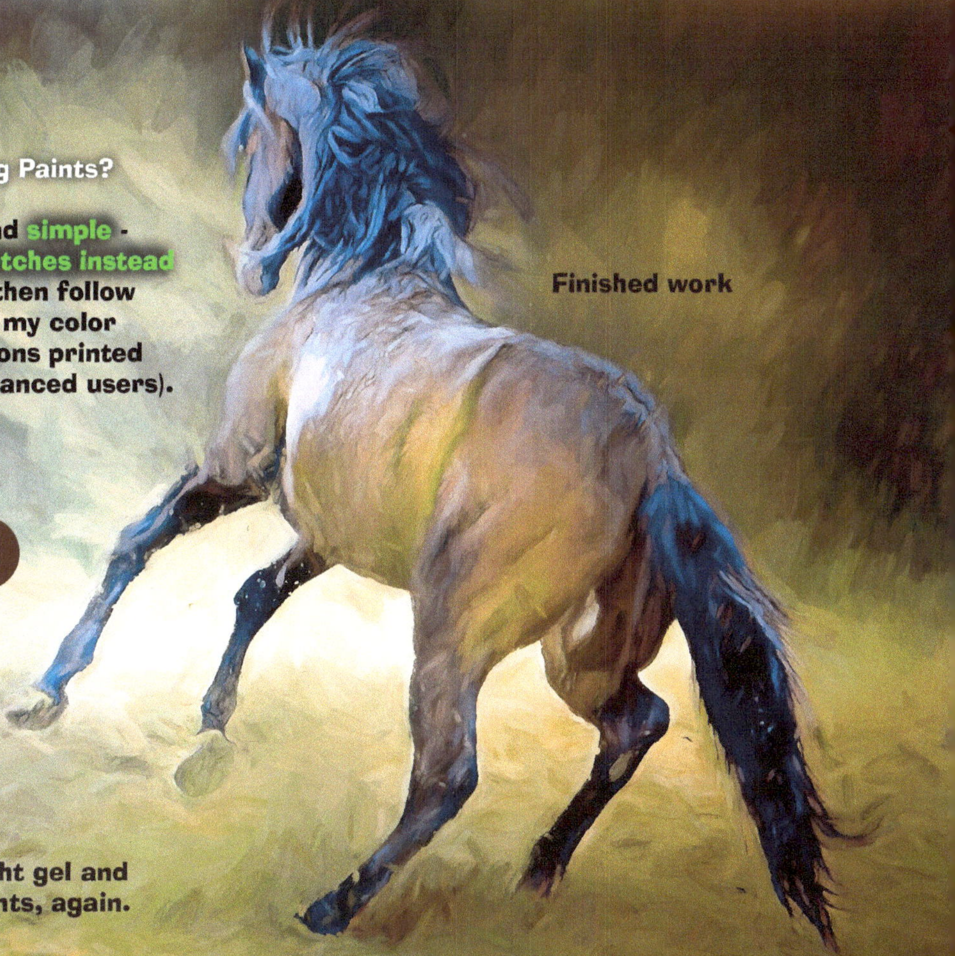

Finished work

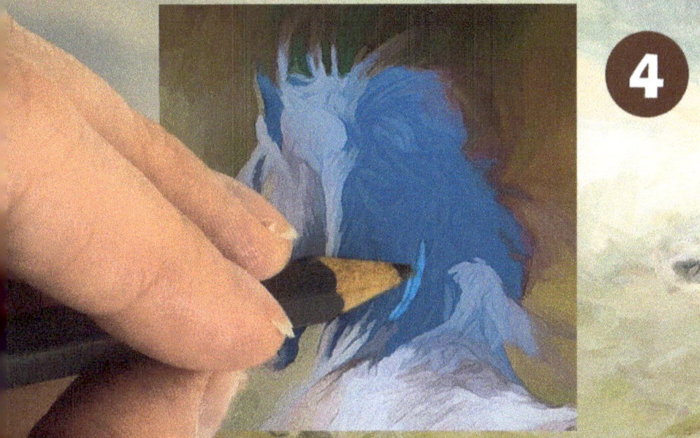

We add some details using light gel and colored pencils. Then, the paints, again.

About the Variants: You can choose the following books:

Original Art (Color Reference)

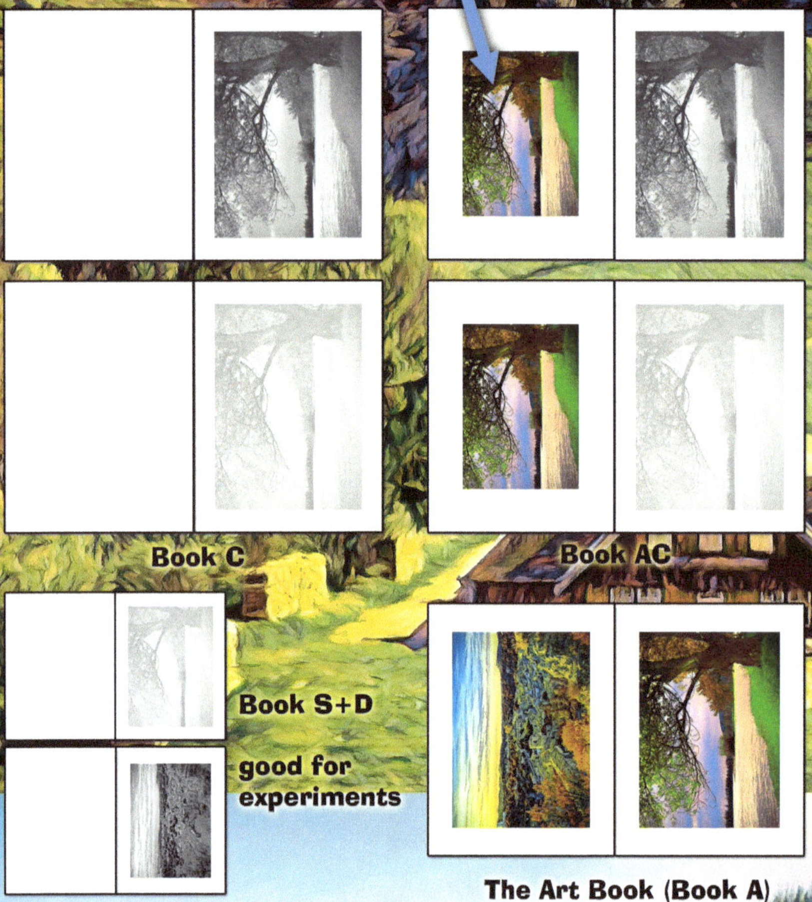

S (Strong) for colored pencils

D (Delicate) for paints

Book C

Book AC

Book S+D good for experiments

The Art Book (Book A)

Coming Soon:

Edu Art for Little Kids

(An Educational Series)

Become a Painter - an Educational Series.
Idea & text & illustrations by: Lech Balcerzak
Raw pics (inc. girl under tree) by: Mimzy & pixabay.com

www.ingramcontent.com/pod-product-compliance
Lightning Source LLC
Chambersburg PA
CBHW040421220526
45473CB00004B/1313
9781720023296